APR '98

COLUMBIA COLLEGE
C1 V 0
372.13T282E
E| WE

C0-DKM-567

Elementary Art Games and Puzzles

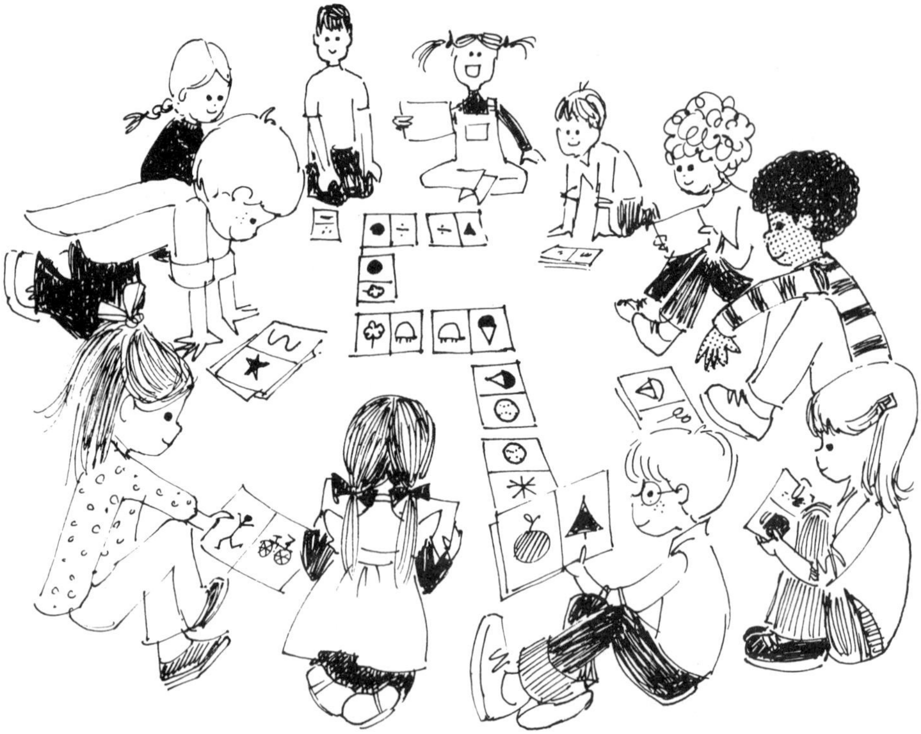

Elementary Art Games and Puzzles

LIBRARY
OF
COLUMBIA COLLEGE
CHICAGO, ILLINOIS

by Florence Temko

*illustrated by Florence Temko
and Sandra Denis*

Parker Publishing Company, Inc.   West Nyack, N.Y.

© 1982, *by*

Florence Temko

All rights reserved. No part of this book may be reproduced or transmitted in any form or by any means, electronic or mechanical, including photocopying, recording, or by any information storage and retrieval system, without permission in writing from the publisher, except where specifically stated in the text.

372.13 T282e

Temko, Florence.

Elementary art, games and puzzles

Library of Congress Cataloging in Publication Data

Temko, Florence.
   Elementary art games and puzzles.

   Includes index.
   1. Educational games—Handbooks, manuals, etc.
2. Art—Study and teaching (Elementary)—Handbooks, manuals, etc. I. Title.
LB1029.G3T45   372.13   81-18789
ISBN 0-13-252965-3   AACR2

Printed in the United States of America

About
the
Author

Florence Temko is the author of 18 books on paper arts and folk crafts, which are well represented in school and public libraries, as well as on teachers' private bookshelves. Besides writing books and magazine articles (*Grade Teacher, Crafts Magazine,* New York Sunday *Times*), she is busy conducting hands-on workshops, classes and lectures in educational and industrial settings, including the Metropolitan Museum of Art, New York, and the Children's Museum, Boston. In all these activities she tries to show her readers and audiences that they are capable of creating something just a little different in a way that feels comfortable to them. This philosophy permeates *Elementary Art Games and Puzzles.*

Ms. Temko studied at Wycombe Abbey School, the London School of Economics, and the New School for Social Research in New York. She lives in Lenox, in the Berkshire Hills of Massachusetts, which she considers conducive to writing and where she is involved in community arts activities. She is listed in *Who's Who of American Women.*

About the Artist

Sandra Denis is a graduate of Massachusetts College of Art. Her subsequent career in commercial as well as fine art brought her winning awards in both fields along the way. She brings her experience as an art teacher to illustrating *Elementary Art Games and Puzzles,* which is her second book with Florence Temko.

Foreword

Astute educators have always known that games and puzzles have tremendous value in children's development. The marvelous thing about them is the combination of structure and freedom which they provide. By definition a game's end is uncertain, and each time it is played the results are different. This forces children to switch their mode of thinking from convergent to divergent. Yet one must abide by the rules in order to play. Games are in fact a microcosm of life.

In this book Florence Temko has wisely developed a game approach to art lessons. It is an appropriate marriage since the children are called upon to design the paraphernalia necessary to the whole process. Possibilities are virtually unlimited, and children with a wide range of abilities can participate successfully.

Additionally the author has described and illustrated these projects with clarity and charm. In many instances the ideas are open ended and can easily be integrated into the regular curriculum. With a modicum of intelligence and flexibility the elementary classroom teacher can use these activities as viable lesson plans; as exciting alternatives to routine methods of teaching. They provide the structure needed for starting and addressing the goals basic to elementary art education: the development within learners of skills in decision-making and creative problem-solving—essential for survival in contemporary society.

Winifred B. Bell
Art Coordinator
Pittsfield Public Schools
Pittsfield, Massachusetts

To Teddy,
who loves art, plays games, and solves puzzles.

ACKNOWLEDGMENT AND THANKS TO:

- Winifred B. Bell, Art Coordinator, Pittsfield Public Schools, Massachusetts
- Lorraine Lauzon, Art Teacher, Berkshire Museum, Pittsfield
- Lillian Sustick, Kindergarten Teacher, Tinton Falls, New Jersey
- The staff of the Lenox Library, Massachusetts
- Bishop Museum, Hawaii
- Crocodile Puzzle inspired by William Accorsi, Artist and Sculptor
- Ronald Temko for photographs

Introduction

"Help!" cries the classroom teacher. "What am I going to do for art tomorrow?" And the answer is... "Games."

This book presents almost 60 games and puzzles that your students can produce as interesting art and craft projects.

- They can use construction paper and glue to design board games such as woven checkerboards in different sizes and colors.
- They can search out colors and shapes in a treasure hunt.
- They can make bannerlike wall games from felt or oaktag, or even from scrap materials if your budget is stretched.
- They can design headdresses for a play they dream up about outer space.
- They can cut puzzles from cardboard and challenge their classmates to solve them.
- They can construct markers from clay.

As students believe games are fun, they respond imaginatively to all the activities, which are, nevertheless, carefully designed to stimulate visual and tactile experiences. The projects include age-old games as well as others newly invented for this volume. They provide a source of tested recipes of necessary art and craft techniques to which your students add their own ingredients of ideas. Playfulness helps to release artistic instincts which are often deeply buried.

A teacher once said to me: "The craft books you write provide just the kind of ideas teachers are always looking for, but the best part is the excitement they bring into the classroom. Students become enthusiastic as the tables fill up with their colorful con-

9

structions. A truly favorable environment for self-expression develops." In "Games and Puzzles" you will find clearly described art activities that will help you provide stimulation for your students, even if you feel art is not your strong point.

Games have been played since the beginning of history and seem to fulfill a deep human need. After the games are made in the art period you can extend their usefulness for enrichment in language development, math and social sciences, if you wish. Suggestions for this type of integration are given throughout the book, in keeping with current educational philosophy that games are a positive part of the curriculum from kindergarten through college, in spite of the increased emphasis being placed on basics.

Pick a game and you'll be all set for tomorrow.

ORGANIZATION OF EACH PROJECT

Each project is loosely organized in the following manner:

Title

The titles are designed to tell you, the teacher, something about the project, but are also worded to appeal to your students.

Grade Level

At the beginning of each project suitable grade levels are suggested, but these levels are not hard and fast. You know your class best, and a project not specifically recommended for your grade may just fit your needs.

Introduction

A few paragraphs tell you about the art project, about the game which is the outcome of the art work, and what special skills are being developed. You will also find some information about alternative materials you might want to consider and other remarks of a general nature.

Materials

The listing of materials includes necessary tools. Only commonly available materials are required, mostly newsprint, drawing and construction papers, tempera paints, crayons, felt-tip pens, cardboard, and occasionally styrofoam.

If you have access to other school supplies or household and industrial leftover materials of any kind, incorporate them in the projects. Obviously it is impossible to specify them, but they are wonderful sources of stimulation. In fact, students should be encouraged to use all kinds of scraps for decorations.

How to Make the Game

Step-by-step directions for the art project are given. You may find this section divided into different subheadings.

How to Play the Game

Specific instructions on how to play the game are provided, including the rules.

With board games it is most important to spend class time on the art project. The games can be played in free time or at home.

Variations

Here are just a few suggestions on how you may be able to adapt the basic games to your needs and integrate them into other areas of study, whether social studies, math or reading. Of course, you and your students will come up with many ideas of your own on the spur of the moment. After all, imagination is the name of the game.

HELPFUL HINT

It is recommended that you read through the whole project before proceeding.

ABOUT MATERIALS

Newsprint and Drawing Paper

These, of course, are your good old standbys.

Construction Paper

In addition to the most commonly used size, 9" x 12" (22.5 x 30 cm), try to acquire the larger size 12" x 18" (22.5 x 30 cm) as well.

Cardboard

Whenever cardboard is specified you can use posterboard, also called railroad board or showcard, which comes in a large selection of colors. It is available from school supply catalogs, local art stores, and even supermarkets and five-and-tens. Oaktag, also called tag board, is strong and smooth yet much less expensive than posterboard, and will do just as well in most instances. In weight and thickness it approximates postcards, but it comes only in cream color.

Corrugated Cardboard

Depending on your budget, you can buy corrugated cardboard through your school supplier or raid your local supermarket. Collapse grocery boxes and then cut out the flat areas with a craft knife.

Clay

Clay is suggested for "The Great Train Robbery" and for making markers. Two types of clay are probably best, unless a kiln is available to you: modeling clay which can be reused and self-hardening clay which does not need to be fired.

Paint

Poster paints are of course most widely available in schools and are least expensive. They are also called tempera paints.

ABOUT MEASUREMENTS

All dimensions are given in inches, followed in parentheses by metric measurements. In order to avoid awkward fractions the two sets of measurements may not always be equal, but either set will work satisfactorily.

HOW TO CUT

Many teachers are not aware that cutting straight lines and curves involves different techniques.

No special instructions are needed for straight cutting, but when cutting curves, move the paper, not the scissors. This is the rule:

WHEN CUTTING CURVES, MOVE THE HAND HOLDING THE PAPER; HOLD THE HAND WITH THE SCISSORS STILL.

ART TIME OR GAME TIME?

As you start using the ideas in this book, you will find that some games are an integral part of the art activity, while with others only the construction of the game has artistic benefits.

Of course your students will want to play the games, but in order to spend the limited amount of time allotted to art most creatively, try to defer pure game playing to other times. Have the games handy when students have finished assignments early or during other free periods, or suggest that they play at home.

Florence Temko

Contents

4 Wall Games 105

Games that can decorate your walls

5 How to Jiggle Without a Saw 119

Jigsaw puzzles and mazes

6 You Got Me! 141

Puzzles and games of skill

Elementary Art
Games
and Puzzles

Chapter 1

1 2 3

Up~and~About Games

4

7 6 5

8 9 10

Games involving physical activity

1.

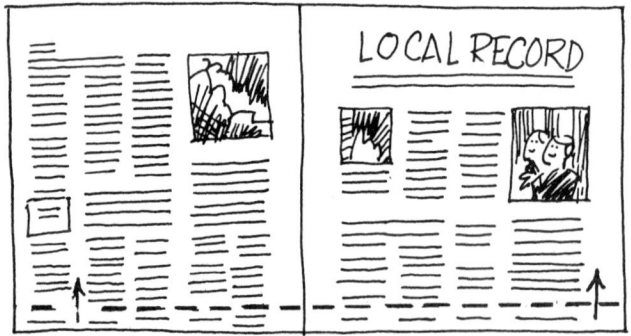

2.

Creatures from Outer Space

For this game your class turns newspapers into headgear for creatures from outer space. A simple cylinder serves as the foundation for decorating, and the art period culminates in a parade or race.

Creating imaginative hats helps to release artistic impulses. When children wear headgear they have made themselves, they play out different roles in their fantasy worlds, which may be therapeutic.

MATERIALS

Newspaper, full size, approx-
   imately 29" x 23" (70 x 58 cm)
Scissors
Cellophane tape or glue
Crayons or paints

TEACHER PREPARATION

1. Cut off about 5" (12 cm) along the length of the paper. Older students can do this themselves.

MAKING THE HATS

First demonstrate making the basic hat in front of your class and then let your students make their own.

2. Fold up a 2" (5 cm) cuff on the long side of the paper.

3. Roll the paper into a cylinder. Overlap the edges and tuck one side into the turned-up cuff. The size can be adjusted to fit the individual child's head.

4. The hat holds together by itself but may be taped or glued.

3.

VARIATIONS

Double Strength: The basic hat can be made from double sheets of newspaper.

Coloring: Let students color hats with crayons or paints before Step 4 is done.

Attachments: Let students roll, crush and shape pieces of newspaper and glue them to the basic hat. Nothing is too outrageous for creatures from outer space.

Pleating: Pleat paper horizontally before rolling it into a cylinder, making pockets to stick things in.

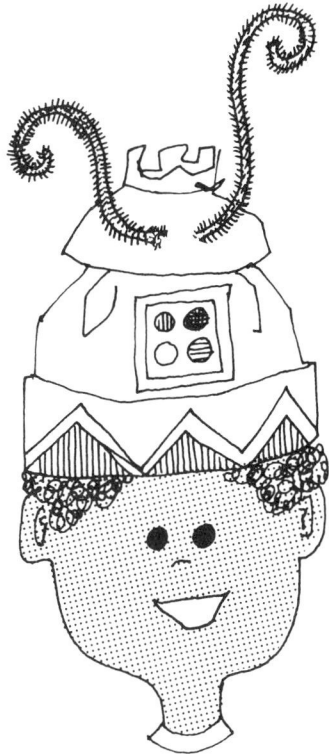

HOW TO PLAY GAMES

For younger students: Have a parade in which they can show off their headgear.

For older students: Divide the class into two groups. Make two obstacle courses by placing perhaps four or five hats in a line, representing space stations. The two groups race each other, weaving in and out between the hats, by placing one foot directly in front of the other, heel to toe. Conduct it like a relay race, with each member of the group touching the next person to start him/her off on the next round.

Storytelling game: Select one student to wear his/her hat. Other students take turns in making up a fantastic story based on the look of the hat:

First student: "The person is trapped in a cave on a distant planet."

Second student: "He[she] collects dewdrops in the cuff of the hat."

Third student: "This energizes the red circle."

Fourth student: "With the power of the red circle.." etc.

Students have to observe closely, yet can let their imaginations run.

After a few turns, or when the story seems to have run its course, select another wearer and begin a new story.

Hopping and Scotching About

Students draw hopscotch games on paper and fill in the whole area with colorful designs. Later they can chalk similar full-size hopscotch games in the school yard. They gain experience in transferring drawings from one size to another, and also have to be able to visualize whether or not their games are practical.

Tell the students that they will be working in the tradition of "sidewalk painters," who used chalk to draw portraits of people, landscapes, and many other subjects on the sidewalk. These chalk paintings were admired by passers-by, who rewarded the painters with money. In the next rain, the paintings were washed away.

MATERIALS

Drawing paper
Crayons or colored pencils
Colored chalks
Pebbles

THE ART PROJECT

1. Draw a regular hopscotch pattern on the blackboard. Explain the rules (given below) as some students may not know them, but do not want to admit it.
2. Now ask students to fill a hopscotch with fanciful designs. All the blocks must be filled in completely with numerals and decorations done in crayons or colored pencils.
3. When they have completed a regular hopscotch, ask the students whether they think hopscotch could be played on different

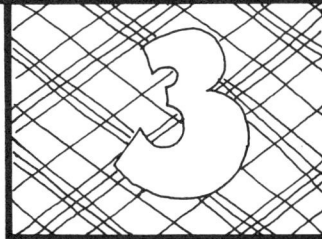

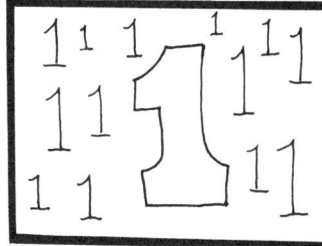

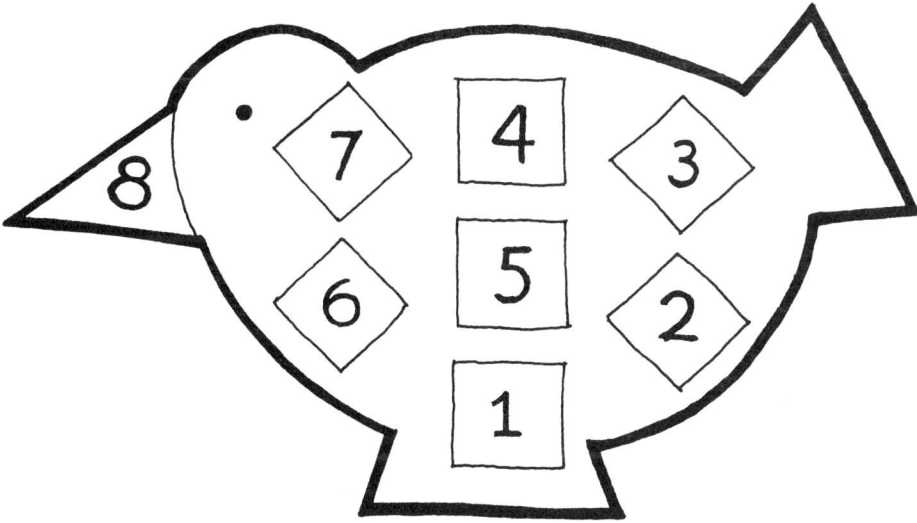

patterns. Let them design as many games as they like (within reason), creating totally different jumping patterns. Two examples are given, one showing faces and the other one contained in the outline of a bird.

4. On a nice day hold art class in the school yard and let students use colored chalk to transfer their hopsctoch games to the blacktop. Here again all the blocks must be completely filled in. Students can repeat previous designs or create entirely new ones.

THE RULES OF HOPSCOTCH

Hopping sequence:

- On one foot hop on square 1, then square 2, then square 3.
- With both feet jump on squares 4 and 5, one foot in each.
- Hop on square 6 with one foot.
- Jump on squares 7 and 8, one foot in each.
- Jump, turning around as you do, landing on squares 7 and 8 again but facing in the opposite direction.
- Hop with one foot on square 6.
- Jump with both feet—one on square 4 and one on square 5.
- Hop with one foot on to square 3, then square 2, then square 1.

Pebbling: But there is the pebble! On each round you throw the pebble on one number and then, still standing on the preceding square, bend down to pick it up.

In the first round the pebble is thrown on #1, on the next round on #2, etc.

Winning: Each player tries to complete all eight rounds without an error. If a player makes a mistake anywhere—by landing with both feet, or forgetting to pick up the pebble—the next person takes a turn. Whoever manages to go eight rounds first wins.

VARIATIONS

There are many variations on the theme; some are already known to the children, but you should encourage them to invent rules of their own.

Olympic High Hurdles

When classes have been confined to the indoors because of bad weather, jumping over hurdles can get rid of some excess energy. In this art project three-dimensional hurdles are formed from flat pieces of cardboard and decorated. In the game the children jump over the hurdles.

MATERIALS

Grocery boxes
Drawing and coloring materials
Cellophane tape
For the teacher: craft knife
Optional: a spinner with six num-
   bers or a 6-pip dice

TEACHER PREPARATION

Collect several cardboard grocery boxes and cut the four sides into flat pieces with a craft knife. The final sizes will vary, of course, and the edges do not have to be ruler straight. Prepare at least one piece of cardboard for each student.

Explain that everybody is going to make a hurdle from cardboard. The hurdles will be placed on the floor and everybody will jump over them.

HOW TO MAKE THE HURDLES

1. Demonstrate by folding a piece of cardboard in half and putting it on a flat surface. If it spreads apart and does not stay upright, pull the bottom edges toward each other and hold them in place with cellophane tape. Suggest that the class should decide on what kind of race is to be held, and talk about different types,

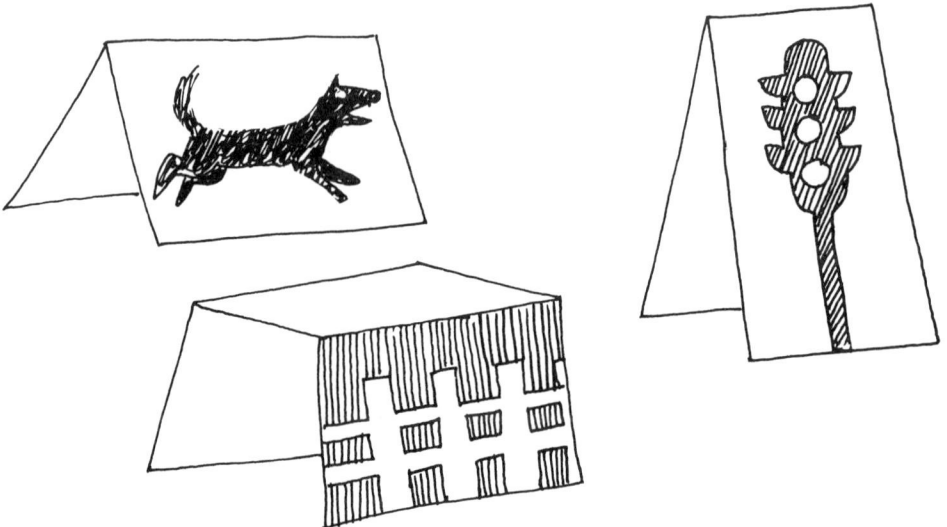

some of which students may have seen: cross country, roller skating, jogging, skiing. Olympic high hurdles and bicycle and horse racing may have been seen on TV. What kinds of obstacles are encountered in these races?

2. Give each child a piece of cardboard. Demonstrate that the cardboard bends cleanly only in the direction of the corrugated lines. Children are to fold the cardboard in half and draw pictures on both sides of the hurdle, illustrating obstacles that may be encountered in the selected race: a traffic light; a dog running across the road; a fallen tree on a ski course; wooden hurdles in a horse race; hills in a bicycle race; etc. The picture can be made as elaborate as the children like.

HOW TO PLAY THE GAME

For kindergarten and first grade: Place the hurdles around the room. Children form a line and jump over the hurdles.

Race game for second and third grade: For a more competitive game, imagine the floor as a board and the children as markers. Four or more players participate at a time.

1. Before beginning the game, each player whirls the spinner or throws the dice to determine who has the highest score and becomes the first player. If two players throw the same highest number, they take another turn. The player with the second highest throw becomes the second player, and so on.

2. A non-player whirls the spinner or throws the dice, and each player in turn jumps over as many hurdles as indicated and then stays there.

3. The first person to go all around the course wins.

VARIATIONS

Other rules: Some classes may enjoy making up their own rules, some of which they may have encountered on regular board games. For example: Lose a turn at certain hurdles, perhaps at a traffic light. Or a player cannot jump over the last hurdle unless he/she gets an exact throw.

Outdoor game: The game can also be played in the school yard. The game can be lengthened by counting an extra space between each hurdle.

Stick-Em-Ups

Students make drawings which they stick on the back of someone else, who has to guess what it is. Suggestions are given for different ways of playing, depending on the age group.

MATERIALS

Drawing paper
Pencils, crayons, or felt-tip pens
Invisible cellophane tape

THE PROJECT

1. Cut the drawing paper into a convenient size, about 6" x 9" (15 x 22 cm).
2. Give each student a piece of paper on which he or she is to make a detailed drawing of an object. Make a few suggestions which include a variety of categories: a bug, a computer, a store, a television personality.
3. Ask students to stick their drawings on someone else's back with the invisible type of cellophane tape that leaves no mark on clothing when removed.

HOW TO PLAY THE GAME

Divide the class into pairs and have them stick drawings on each other's backs. First one of them tries to guess what the drawing on his/her back represents by asking questions which can be answered only with yes and no. When the child has guessed correctly, the roles of artist and guesser are reversed.

VARIATIONS

All together now: The game can also be played by having each person stick a drawing on the back of his/her neighbor. The whole class moves about the room freely and asks questions of anyone, which again can elicit only yes or no.

For kindergarten and lower grades: Rather than pin drawings on their backs, students hold up their own drawings and the whole class guesses what they are.

Draw-ins: In another variation the guesser not only has to find out the object, but also has to make a drawing of it. Afterward point out how differently two people can draw the same object.

Race: To make the game more challenging for older students, have a race between two groups. The group that guesses all the drawings in the shortest period of time is the winner.

Specifics: You can set certain objectives for the drawings: use two complementary colors only; draw an object in perspective; draw animals; select a subject being studied in reading or social science class; or take another approach, such as illustrating something from a particular country.

Self-stick labels: You can use peel-off labels, which serve as nametags at conferences.

Treasure Hunt

A treasure hunt around the classroom sounds like just plain fun, but in the process children learn about colors. They look for objects in a specific color. Kindergartners and first graders concentrate on primary colors (red, yellow and blue) and secondary colors (green, orange and violet). Second and third graders, who already know colors, become aware of different values and hues.

After the treasure hunt, children draw objects in one color only. If red was the choice, they draw hearts, Santa Claus, a geranium, and other red things.

MATERIALS

Drawing paper
Poster paints

HOW TO GO ON A TREASURE HUNT

1. Tell the children they are going on a funny kind of treasure hunt, looking around the room to find things in one special color. First let the class decide which color to look for. You could take five pieces of paper, smear each with a different color, fold up the papers, fan them out in your hand, and let a child pick one. Let's say it's pink. Children take turns naming something pink that they see: a piece of construction paper, something on an illustration on the wall, a house seen through the window. They can even open a book.

2. The second part of the game is to paint different things in just that color on a sheet of white paper. The children can include

some of the things they have seen in the room, as well as things they remember, such as a strawberry ice cream cone or a pink dress.

VARIATIONS

Values and hues: For children who know colors already, prepare for the treasure hunt by asking the class to mix any two paint colors together and describe the results. Yellow and blue turn into green; red and yellow make orange; green and blue may turn into mostly green or blue, depending on the mixture. After a while you can summarize that when a little bit of another color is added, the original color changes in *hue*. When either black or white is added, the hue stays the same, but the *value* changes, the color becoming greyer or brighter.

After this exercise let children go on a treasure hunt and compare two similar colors with each other, saying why they think they are different. "This purple has more blue in it. The other purple has more red." "Here are two red books. How are they different?" "One is lighter and the other is darker." Many children are able to cope with this seemingly advanced concept because they can look for the same color they have already used in mixing two paints.

Go Fish!

Your class first learns to make origami fish from colored paper and then plays a game fishing for them.

Origami is the art of folding paper without cutting or gluing, which aids coordination between eye and hand. Before instructing your class, you should become thoroughly familiar with the five simple steps that produce the fish.

You need 4" (10 cm) paper squares, which you can cut on a guillotine-type paper cutter from colored art paper, discarded colored flyers, or computer paper.

Suggestions are given to make the game interesting for different grade levels.

MATERIALS

Colored paper cut into 4" (10 cm)
   squares
Four dowel sticks, approximately
   ¼" (½ cm) in diameter
String
Scissors
Christmas ornament hangers or
   wire
Grocery box
Straight pin

HOW TO MAKE THE FISH

1. Fold paper square on the diagonal. (For younger children say: "Let the bottom corner kiss the top corner.") Then UNFOLD the paper.

2. Fold the outer EDGES to the center fold, as shown by the dotted lines and arrow.

3. Fold the tip BACKWARDS as shown by the broken line.

4. Fold the paper in half lengthwise.

5. Fold up the tail at an angle, as shown.

6. With the straight pin pierce a hole at the top of fish and attach a Christmas hook or piece of wire bent into shape.

Fish

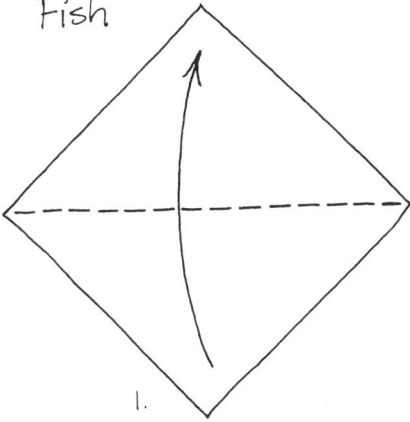

1.

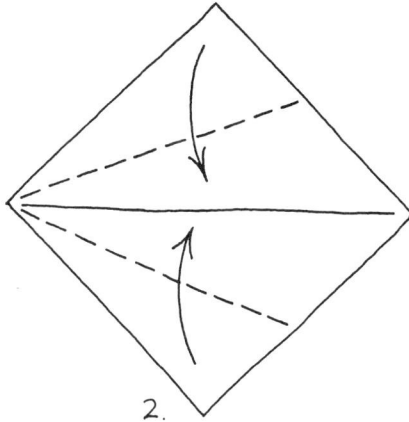

2.

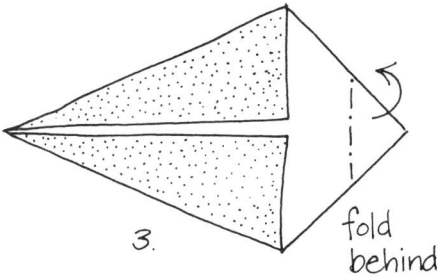

3.   fold behind

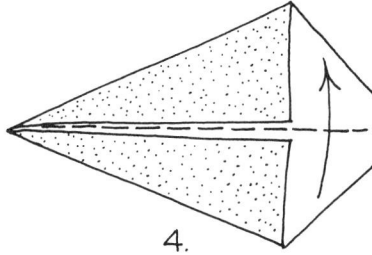

4.

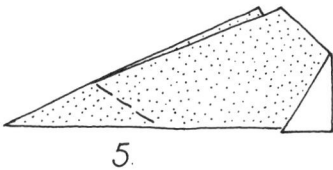

5.

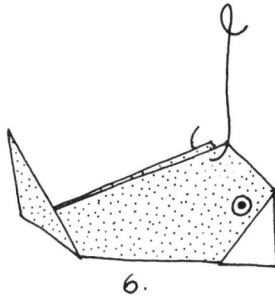

6.

Another Fish

1.

2.

3.

4.

5.

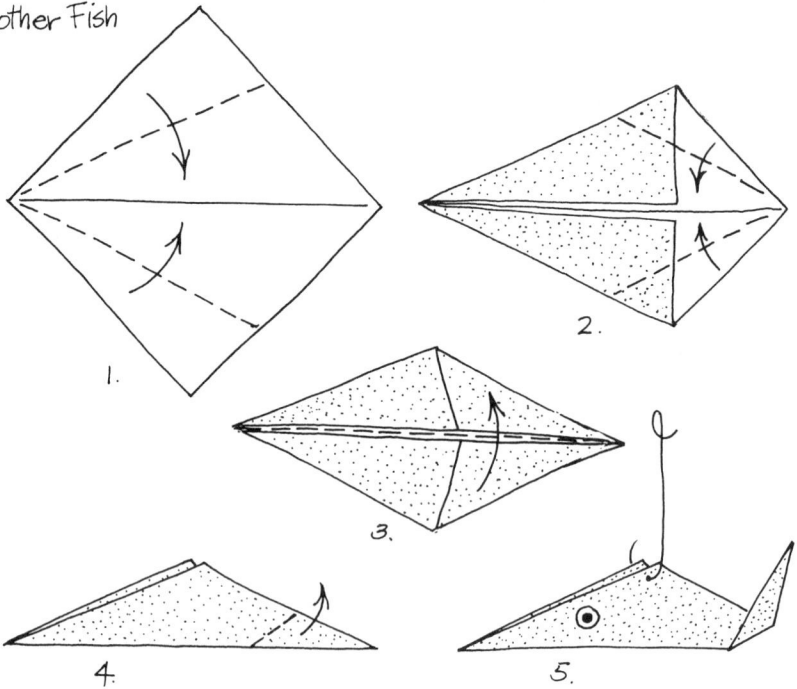

HOW TO MAKE THE FISHING ROD

7. Cut four pieces of string approximately 20" (45 cm) long. Tie one end of each piece to the end of a dowel stick. Tie the other end of the string to the closed part of a Christmas ornament hanger. If they are not available, bend a 2½" (6 cm) piece of wire into the shape shown in the drawing.

HOW TO PLAY THE GAME

Put a lot of fish into the grocery box. Four children at a time try to hook the fish. The game is over when all the fish have been lifted out of the box. The one with the most fish is declared the winner.

VARIATIONS

For grades 4-6: The game can be made more difficult by placing the grocery box at eye level so that players cannot see the fish. This can be achieved by having the players kneel around a table. Alternatively, players could be blindfolded. If you think your students would find this game too childish, go on to some of the other suggestions.

Scoring: Make fish in different colors, which carry different values.

Pink shark   —5 points
Bluefish   —3 points
Gray sardine—1 point

New designs: After students know how to make the fish, ask them to change the design and fold their own fish. Suggest that they try to create different silhouettes: short and squat; long and pointed. The folding sequence for another fish is given in the accompanying drawings as an example.

Tropical fish mobile: Make a mobile of fish in brilliant colors. This makes a nice tie-in for studies of tropical fish which can lead to another art project: coloring paper fish with patterns imitating nature. As still another art project, assemble folded fish into an underwater scene.

Storage: The pieces of the game can be kept in the grocery box for future use.

Follow-the-Leader

In this variation on a traditional game the leader creases a piece of paper instead of performing the usual physical actions. The game is intended to help your students discover how paper can be manipulated. It follows very nicely after the previous project ("Go Fish!") as your students will already have some experience in folding paper.

"Follow-the-Leader" is divided into two parts: "Follow-the-Teacher" when you are the leader, and "Follow-Me" when a student becomes the leader.

Pre-cut origami squares featured in school supply catalogs are best to use. Otherwise you can cut almost any kind of paper into 6" (15 cm) squares on a guillotine-type paper cutter. Colored art paper, duplicating paper, used flyers are all suitable.

MATERIALS

6" (15 cm) paper squares

HOW TO PLAY "FOLLOW THE TEACHER"

1. Hand out paper squares and tell the class you are going to play "Follow-the-Leader." Some will have a chance at being the leader later on, but first they are to follow everything you do with a piece of paper.
2. In the illustrations presented here you will find two folding sequences to show your class:
   • first sequence—ice cream cone, kite, diamond;
   • second sequence—picnic table, stool.

1.

2.

3.

4.

5.

ice cream
cone

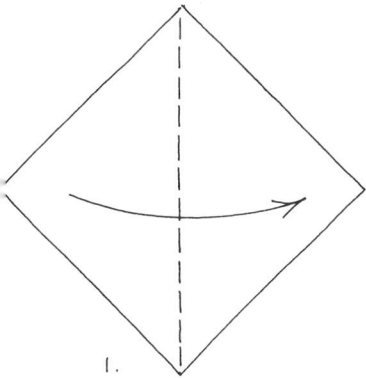

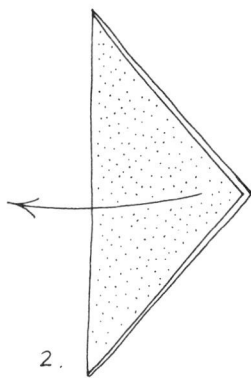

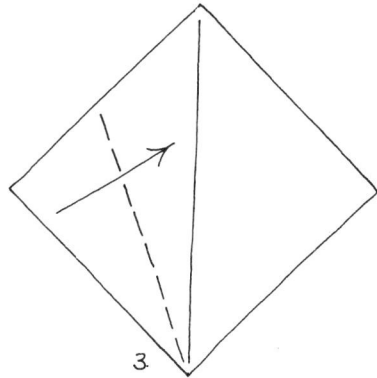

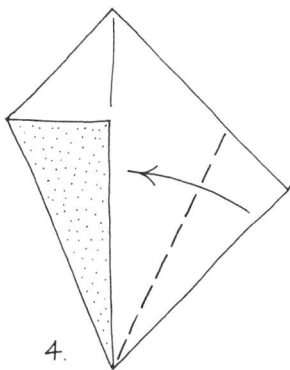

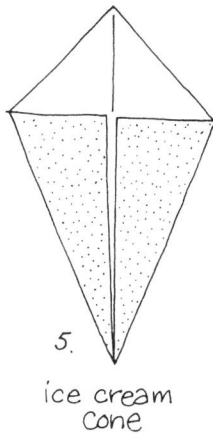

turn
paper
over →

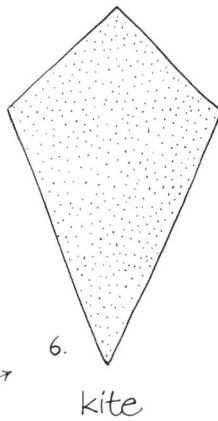

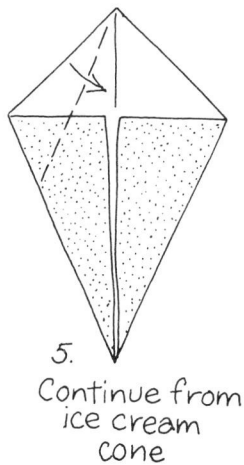

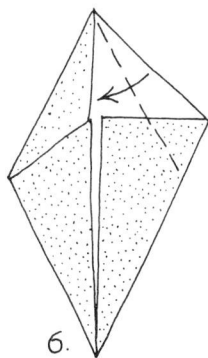

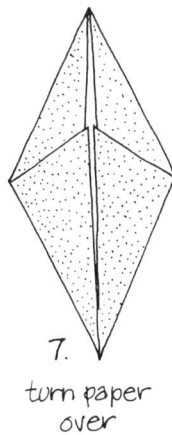

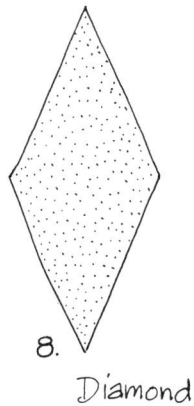

6.

kite

5.

Continue from
ice cream
cone

6.

7.

turn paper
over

8.

Diamond

Table

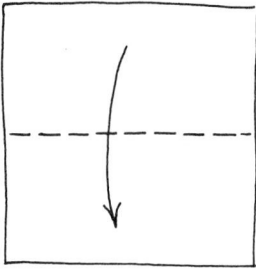

1.

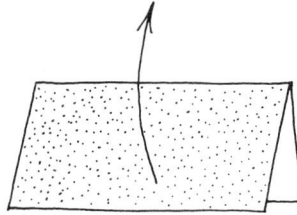

2.

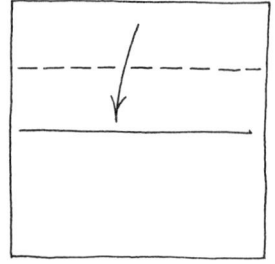

3.

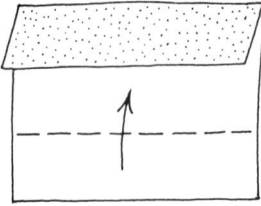

4.

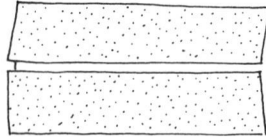

5. Loosen the flaps and stand up

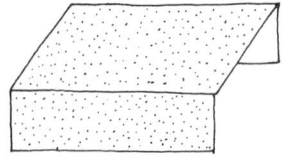

6. Table

Stool

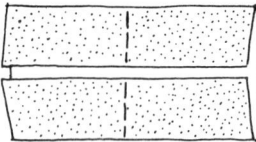

7. Fold and unfold

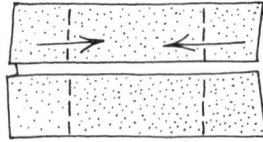

8.

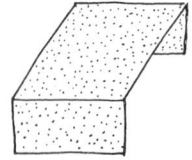

9. Stool

Be sure to familiarize yourself with the separate steps before you give instructions to your class.

HOW TO PLAY "FOLLOW-ME"

1. You or the class selects a leader. The leader takes a piece of paper and creases it once. Everybody else imitates. The leader then makes another crease on the same square and everyone repeats the step. The result does not have to look like anything at all, but you should help the leader fold the paper in half, edge to the middle, or use some other definite guidelines. You can verbalize what you see the child is doing.

2. After six or more creases have been made, elect another leader and repeat the game.

VARIATIONS

Experimenting: To stimulate their imagination, encourage students to call out what the piece of paper looks like when a new crease is added: a fish, a dog, a cloud, a tree, a flag, whatever. Not every change will suggest something.

More origami: Fourth graders and up often enjoy learning origami from a book in their free time. Encourage them to borrow books on the subject from the local library or to seek out someone in the community who does origami.

Animal Toss

Each student designs a papier mache animal with a trunk, nose, horn, or other feature that sticks out prominently. The completed animals are used in a game of ring toss.

Papier mache is a wonderfully inexpensive medium to use in experiencing molding in three dimensions, and your students will love it. Some teachers believe papier mache is a complicated process, but it is actually very easy to concoct, and almost any kind of consistency is acceptable. Instructions for making papier mache from scratch with newspaper and plastic wallpaper paste are given here. This is marketed as Art Paste or Metylan and is quite inexpensive. Wheat paste, which was used traditionally, is still cheaper, but is more troublesome and not worth the price saving. You can also use white glue diluted—one cup of glue to three cups of water. If your budget allows, you can buy prepared papier mache which is marketed in school supply catalogs under such names as Celluclay or Shreddi-mix.

A few days before you are planning to do this project, ask your class to bring in plastic throwaway bowls and containers, for holding the glue mix, as well as cardboard tubes from paper towels, toilet paper and other paper products, for basic forms.

MATERIALS

Newspapers
Powdered plastic wallpaper
   paste
Water
Plastic throwaway bowls and
   containers

Cardboard tubes
Cellophane tape
Scissors
Tempera paints and brushes

HOW TO MAKE THE ANIMALS

(Protect working surfaces with several layers of newspaper.)

1. Tear newspapers into pieces approximately 1½″ (4 cm) square. A good way to do this is to tear the paper into long strips with the grain, meaning in the direction in which the paper tears most easily. Then tear the strips into smaller pieces, which can be quite irregular.
2. Form the body of the animal by crushing a sheet of newspaper into a tight ball. For the head, legs, tails, and ears, attach, with cellophane tape, smaller balls of crushed newspaper and pieces of cardboard tubing. One element should stick out prominently and curve upward. It could be a bird's beak, elephant's trunk, bull's horn, monkey's arm, insect antenna, whatever will serve to catch the ring in the game of animal toss.

3. Mix the paste powder with water according to the directions on the box. A little goes a long way. Pour into plastic containers for easy access by small groups of students.

4. Dip torn pieces of paper into the paste and layer them on the forms. Continue adding two or more layers, letting each layer dry before adding the next one.

5. Cover the completed animal with another layer of paste. Let dry.

DECORATING

6. When completely dry the animals can be painted with tempera or acrylic paints.

7. A final glossy coat can be applied with white glue diluted with an equal amount of water.

NEWSPAPER RINGS

8. Roll half a sheet of newspaper, approximately 11" x 14" (27 x 35 cm), diagonally from one corner (see drawing). Rolling the paper over a pencil or a knitting needle may help you to get started. With a small piece of cellophane tape, secure the corner on the outside of the roll.

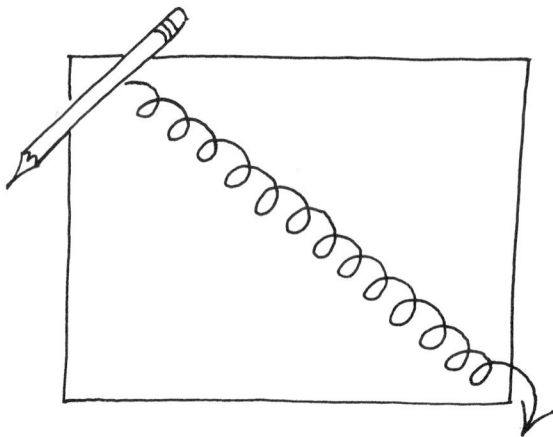

9. Bend the rolled paper into a circle, overlapping the ends and securing them with cellophane tape. Try to make all the rings about the same size, say 3½" (8 cm) diameter.

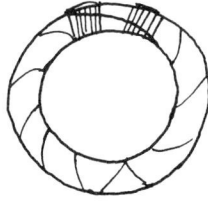

HOW TO PLAY THE GAME

Children, standing a certain distance away, toss the rings onto the nose or other protuberance. They take turns, each one starting off with the same number of rings, let's say five. Whoever lands the greatest number is the winner. If everyone gets all the rings on, increase the distance of the throw.

VARIATIONS

Tissue paper surface: Instead of painting the animals, color them with tissue paper. Dip small pieces of tissue paper into the paste and apply them in the same way as the torn pieces of newspaper were applied.

Rubber rings: Instead of newspaper rings, use rubber rings from preserving jars.

Huge-Imos

For this form of dominoes, pictures are used instead of numbers. Children draw the same picture twice, learning to control design. Playing the game itself sharpens their powers of observation.

MATERIALS

Two pieces of cardboard, 6" x 12"
   (15 x 30 cm), for each student
Crayons

TEACHER PREPARATION

After you have cut the cardboard to size, draw a line down the middle, dividing the pieces into two squares.

If you have more than 20 children, divide the class into two working groups; otherwise the game will become unwieldy.

HOW TO DRAW THE DOMINOES

1. Give each child two pieces of cardboard. Tell the children to draw the same picture on both pieces, but to use up only one square on each. Bold designs of a single thing are best, such as a tree, a rocket, a table, or a person.
2. Put all the designed pieces in a pile and mix them up. Then let each child pick two pieces and draw two pictures that are alike on the empty squares, being sure not to draw the same designs as before.

HOW TO PLAY THE GAME—TWO VERSIONS

Simple version:

1. Several children sit on the floor in a circle. Huge-imos are placed in a pile inside the circle, blank sides up.

2. One huge-imo is placed, drawing side up, in the middle of the circle.

3. Children all pick up a piece from the pile and try to match a drawing to one of the pictures on the huge-imo in the center. Anyone who picks up a matching drawing can start the game. If two children can match the tile in the center, they both put their tiles down. The game continues with the next player on the left taking a turn. If two players were able to begin, any players seated between the two starters are left out in this round. The game continues in clockwise fashion.

4. If a player cannot match a drawing, he/she picks another tile, and if this doesn't match either, the turn passes to the next player. In the end all pieces are used up.

5. The game can be played non-competitively, or the player to place the last huge-imo can be declared the winner.

Traditional version for up to six players:

1. Each child takes three dominoes from the pile.

2. One huge-imo is placed in the center as a starter, drawing up.

3. Anyone who can match the starter drawings begins play, which continues in clockwise fashion. If no one can match them, then determine the first player by having all players guess a number written on a secret piece of paper.

4. The first player takes a piece from the pile. If he/she cannot match it to the starter, the turn passes to the next player, who proceeds in the same way.

5. The first player who disposes of all his/her dominoes is the winner.

HELPFUL HINT

The number of huge-imos in play may vary, depending on the size of your class, which influences how many pieces were produced. If there are a lot, each player can begin with up to six huge-imos instead of three. The rules are intended to be flexible, so that children can learn that rules may be changed, as long as they are agreed on beforehand.

Walkie-Talkie

You want to give your students experience in all kinds of art techniques and in this *wow!* project they are exposed to hard-edge painting. Here it is used to create a walkie-talkie that works.

In hard-edge painting artists produce striped and other precisely defined shapes with the help of masking tape, which is handled in much the same way as it is in painting the edges of walls in your house or painting stripes on a car. Such paintings are usually done on treated canvas, but as this is too costly, you can substitute plastic containers. Although the surfaces are curved, the technique is the same. Ask students to bring in a lot of plain deli containers, margarine bowls, and similar throwaways without printing.

To inspire your students, perhaps your library can supply some books illustrating hard-edge paintings, a term coined in the late 1950's. Frank Stella, Victor Vasarely, and Ellsworth Kelly are well-known artists who have painted in this style.

MATERIALS

2 plain plastic containers
½" (1 cm) masking tape
Poster paints
Brushes
String
Scissors
Craft knife or a nail pushed
    through a cork

Masking tape

Paint in between

HOW TO DECORATE THE CONTAINERS

1. Wind three strips of masking tape all around a plastic container, leaving about ½″ (1 cm) of space in between the strips. Press tape down firmly.

2. Paint the spaces between the tapes in two different colors.

3. Let the paint dry and pull the masking tape off gently, exposing the design. You may want to postpone this operation until the next art period.

4. Containers can also be painted by applying masking tape to define spaces and painting them. Strips can be applied vertically and in short lengths to create more interesting designs. Masking tape can be applied over painted areas, so that empty spaces can be filled in.

HOW TO MAKE THE WALKIE-TALKIE

5. Make a hole in the center of the bottom of the containers. This is best done by heating a nail held in a piece of cork. You may want to take all the containers home with you and do the job on a gas stove. You can also cut a very small square hole with a craft knife.

   EITHER WAY, THIS JOB MUST BE DONE BY AN ADULT.

6. Cut a length of string ten feet or more. Knot the ends inside the containers.

HOW TO USE THE WALKIE-TALKIE

To hold a conversation, one person speaks into a container and the other person holds a container against one ear. The string must be stretched taut.

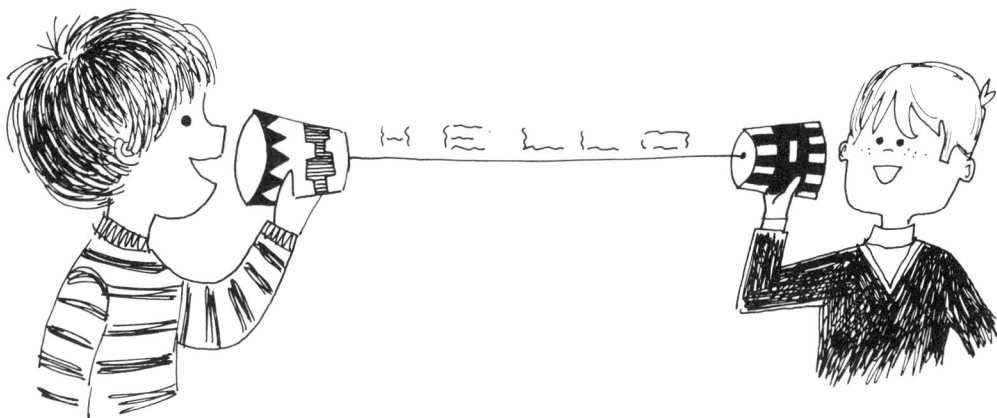

VARIATIONS

Gifts: Quart containers decorated with hard-edge painting make nice vases or flowerpots, useful for gifts on Mother's Day and other occasions.

Flat plastic: Clear plastic floor matting sold by the yard is another material suitable for hard-edge painting. It can be used for gameboards.

Chapter 1 2 3 4 7 6 5 8 9 10

Whirlers

Spinning disks that produce designs and can be used like dice

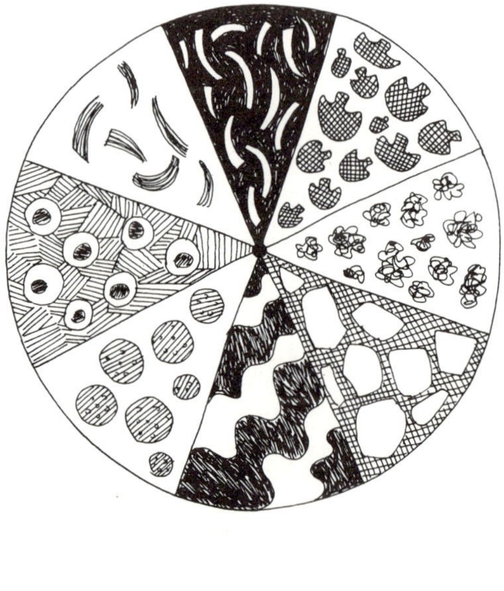

K-Grade 6

Pizza Pie

For this game students decorate a cardboard pizza pie and have to remember how to draw things they have seen many times. They can also use their imagination in making up pizzas that never were and that might not taste very well.

The game, which is played with a spinner, can be used by the lower grades to learn colors and by middle grades to practice addition and multiplication.

MATERIALS

Construction paper, oaktag or
  cardboard
Felt-tip pens or paints
Scissors
Brass two-pronged paper
  fasteners

HOW TO MAKE THE PIZZA

1. Cut the paper into 9" (22 cm) squares
2. Draw a circle as large as possible.
3. Divide the circle into eight pie-shaped wedges.
   a. First draw a vertical line.
   b. Then draw a horizontal line.
   c. Then draw lines in between.

4. Now pretend that each wedge is a different kind of pizza: mushroom, sausage, tomato, peppers, cheese or several combined, and draw them on. Tell students they can use their imaginations. For example a sausage pizza could be drawn with whole sausages or with round sausage slices. Or they could invent totally new kinds.

5. From the leftover construction paper or oaktag, cut an arrow almost as long as the diameter of the pizza. Place it on the pizza and pierce a hold with the point of the scissors through both the arrow and the pizza, making sure it is centered where all the wedges meet.

6. Push a two-pronged brass fastener through the hole and the game is ready to be played.

7. Draw the numbers 1 to 8 on the wedges, in any sequence.

Spinner attached

HOW TO PLAY THE GAME

Any number of players can take turns in spinning the arrow three times and adding up the numbers. Whoever scores highest is the winner.

VARIATIONS

Simplified version: For kindergarten and first grade, prepare a large cardboard pizza pie yourself and have the children use it for learning color. Make each wedge a different color, and prepare a lot of pie-shaped pieces of paper in the same colors. When children spin the arrow, they have to pick up the piece of paper that matches the color of the wedge.

Multiplication: For older students, instead of adding, have them multiply the numbers. The work can be done in their heads or on paper.

Story pizza: To stimulate their imaginations, let students paint a fantastic pizza: a pizza made with candy; a pizza made with butterfly wings; a pizza made with tools.

Another adding game: You or one of the children spin the arrow twice, calling out the numbers. Children add them up in their heads, and the first one to shout out the result scores a point. You write his/her name on a piece of paper, and when the game is over, the child with most points is the winner.

Magic Spinner

The spinner whirls and magic designs appear! What could be more fun than to create unexpected surprises and at the same time learn about kinetic art! There is no mystery about the meaning of kinetic art: it means art in motion. A design changes its appearance either by the work itself moving or by the work remaining still and the beholder moving.

In this project a spinner is whirled and unexpected optical illusions are produced. You may have seem similar effects created at fairs where they never fail to delight and amaze adults as well as children.

Styrofoam trays used for packaging produce and meat are the best material, but fairly stiff paper, index cards, and oaktag can be used satisfactorily. With cardboard the center hole which holds the pin or nail tends to become enlarged, but remedies are suggested. Straight pins are suitable for small models, but T-pins or headed nails about 1½" to 2" (4 to 5 cm) long are better.

Teach the project in its simplest form to any grade but add challenging variations for older students. In any case have enough materials on hand, as students usually want to make several spinners.

MATERIALS

Styrofoam meat trays, index
    cards, or paper of similar
    weight
Straight pins or nails
Scissors
Felt-tip pens or paints

TEACHER PREPARATION

For lower grades prepare step 1 in advance.

HOW TO MAKE THE SPINNER

1. Cut styrofoam, index cards or paper into squares, anywhere between 4" and 8" (10 and 20 cm). Paper cutter helps.
2. Demonstrate making a spinner.
   a. Draw a rough semi-circle on the paper.
   b. Stick a pin in the center and whirl it.
   c. Let class describe what they see: a full circle.
   Now they can't wait to do it themselves.
   Note: Very young students need help with sticking the pin right in the center.
3. If you are using cardboard, the hole may become enlarged after a couple of twirls, inhibiting the action. This can be remedied by putting a small piece of cellophane tape over the head of the pin or nail and also squashing another small piece on the back.

VARIATIONS

Other shapes: Suggest that students should try all kinds of different lines, dots, and shapes, twirling the paper after each addition to see what happens.

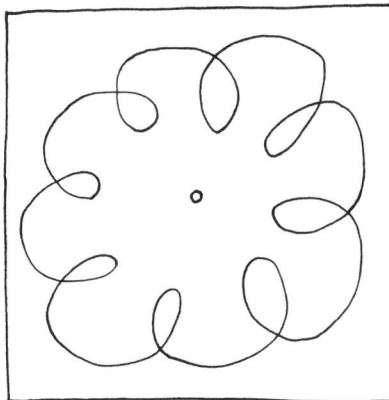

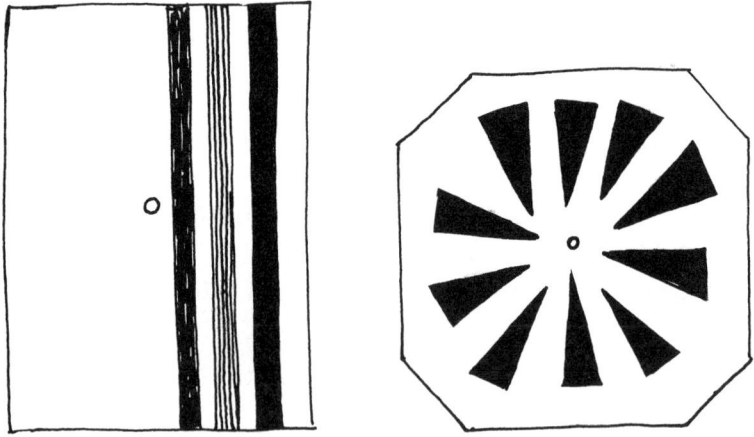

Optical illusion: Let students take turns at whirling each others' spinners and discuss the effect created by different designs. Then let them experiment some more. Does the effect change if the piece of paper is round instead of square?

Paper cut-outs: Instead of paint, glue on colored paper shapes.

Plastic spinners: Use plastic lids from coffee cans, nut cans, etc.

Community projects: Your class could make magic spinners and contribute them to a local bazaar. Or you could set up a booth at a school benefit and provide materials for kids to make them right there and then. Spinners could be made for hospital giveaways to children at Christmas or any time of the year.

Larger spinners: For more substantial models, use regular or corrugated cardboard or larger pieces of styrofoam.

Holiday colors: This project is easily adapted to the seasons by simply choosing holiday colors for the materials.

Spinners As Dice

These spinners are made the same way as the Pizza Pie, but are used instead of dice for other games. They are more versatile than six-pip cube dice, as they can have as few as two numbers or as many numbers as you choose.

MATERIALS

Construction paper, oaktag or
  cardboard
Felt-tip pens
Brass two-pronged paper
  fasteners

HOW TO MAKE THE SPINNERS

1. Cut the paper into a 9″ (22 cm) diameter circle.
2. Divide the circle into as many numbers as seems best for the game to be played. Divide in half for two numbers, into eight wedges for numbers 1-8, or even into 12 or 16 wedges. Spinners for these numbers are made most easily, but there is no reason why you can't have any other numbers, and the wedges do not necessarily have to be the same sizes.
3. Cut an 8″ (20 cm) arrow.
4. Attach the arrow to the center of the paper with the paper fastener.

VARIATION

Paper plates: Use uncoated paper plates to make spinners.

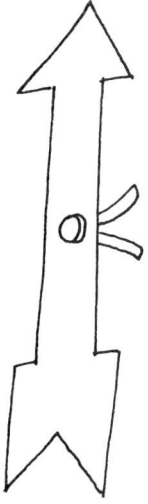

Chapter **1** **2** **3**

Play It Again and Again!

4

7 **6** **5**

8 **9** **10**

How to make exciting board games

ABOUT GAME BOARDS

The materials suggested for making most of the game boards in this chapter are construction paper and posterboard, as they are most widely available in schools. However, boards can be made from corrugated cardboard cut from grocery boxes or from regular cardboard, which will make them much sturdier. If you intend to have the games available for free time play, you can cover them for even longer life with plastic, either acrylic sheeting available by the yard in art stores or self-stick (Con-Tact®) available in variety and hardware stores.

Grades 3-6

Get the Job!

This is an adaptation of Parchisi, which has survived for centuries as the most popular game in India. It is played day in and day out by young and old, rich and poor. Its universality will appeal to your students, especially in this updated version, where four teenagers compete for a newspaper route and the job goes to the winner of the game.

The board is cross shaped, with each arm of the cross divided into 24 small blocks. This simple basic design leaves plenty of blank space for your students to decorate. With the technique of stenciling they can repeat the same motif in all four corners, while learning about symmetry and exploring the kinds of patterns that are most effective for stenciling.

Stenciling is usually done with paint and a stiff brush. Tempera paint is an entirely suitable medium for your students to use in learning the technique, but they will not be able to achieve sharp, clean edges in their designs. Broad felt-tip markers are much easier to use and give good results, but you must consider the expense.

To help your students start right in with the art project without bothering to draw the exacting board, you can duplicate the grids shown on the next page, providing four rectangles for each student.

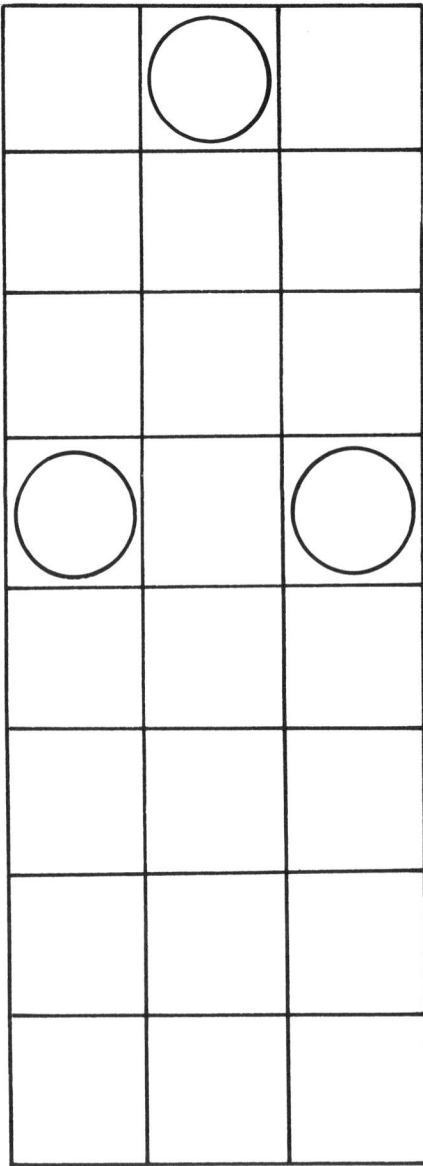

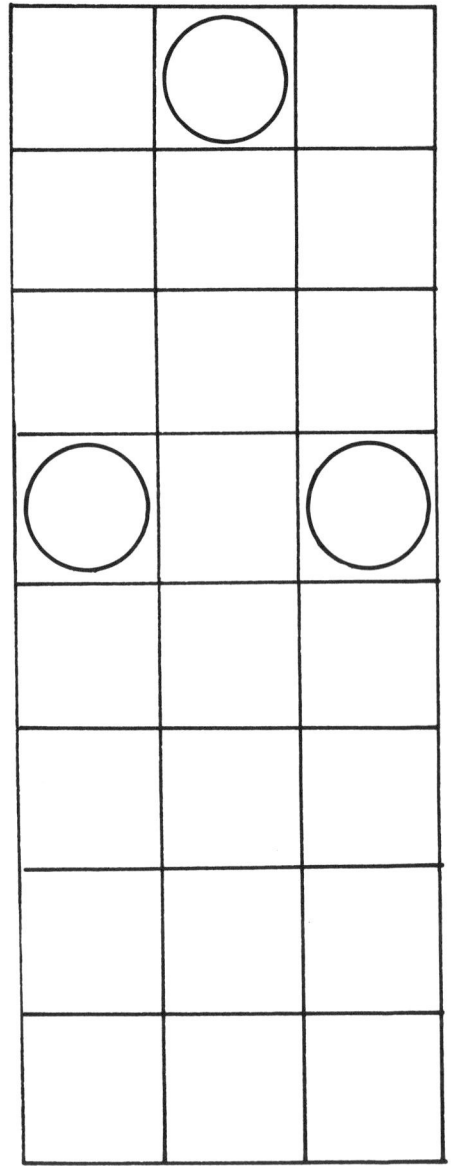

MATERIALS FOR EACH STUDENT

Two duplicates of the gridded
   rectangles shown here
Oaktag, 12″ x 12″ (30 x 30 cm)
4″ (10 cm) squares of oaktag
Newsprint or other paper

Scissors

Tempera paint and stiff brush or
   broad felt-tip pen

4 markers for each player (a
   different color for each player)

2 dice (per game)

HOW TO MAKE THE BOARD

1. Tell students to paste their four gridded rectangles on the large piece of oaktag in a cross shape, either straight or on the diagonal. Make sure the circle in the middle row of the grid is on the outside (show them the drawing).

2. Draw a picture of a newspaper office in the center.

3. The empty spaces are going to be decorated with stenciled designs. (Explain the technique of stenciling, which in this case is to draw a design on a 4" (10 cm) oaktag square, cut out and throw away the scraps, and place the square with its open design on the board. The design is then carefully filled in with tempera paint and the stencil removed.)

HOW TO MAKE DESIGNS FOR STENCILS

4. Now give out small oaktag squares. Ask students to fold them in half and cut away shapes on the folded edge. DO NOT CUT ALL THE WAY ACROSS TO THE OPPOSITE EDGE, as the stencil will fall apart if you do.

5. Let students experiment. First have them make one simple bold outline. They will discover that an outline that begins and ends on the folded edge works. Let them stencil these first attempts on scrap paper to see the effect. They can add details, and they will also discover that half-outlines of trees, flowers and other things work.

6. They can sketch the designs in pencil first, but should not attempt to follow the lines exactly when cutting. When they have evolved a design to their liking, they are ready to decorate the game boards.

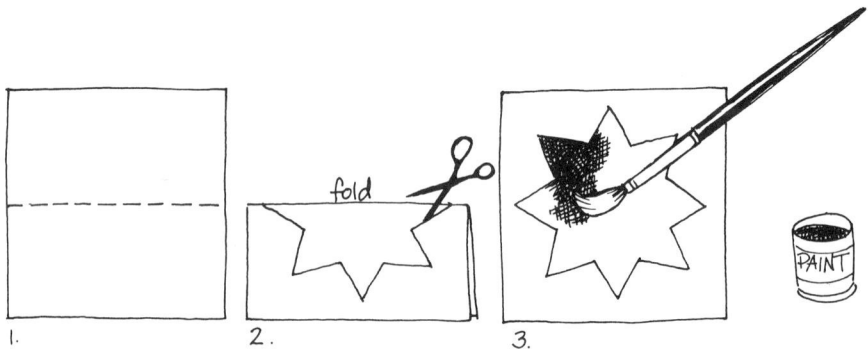

HELPFUL HINTS

Brush paint over the edges of the stencil toward the middle of the cut-out areas.

When using a felt-tip pen, short strokes are better.

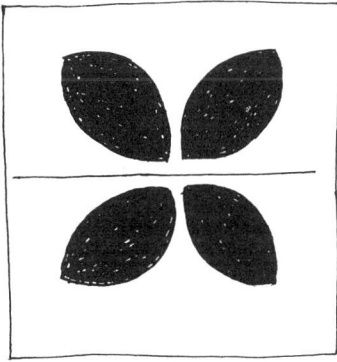

Two leaves almost look like a butterfly

A try at a bicycle wheel

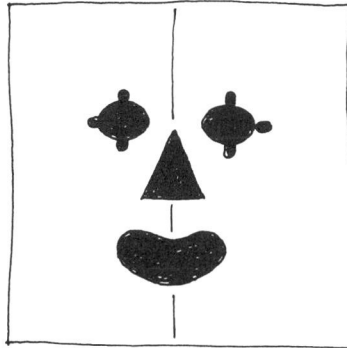

Three arrows form a chevron pattern

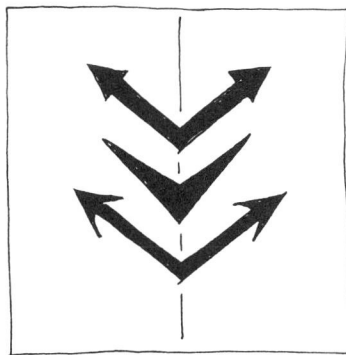

HOW TO PLAY THE GAME

The game can be played by two or four players, each of whom has four markers.

Two players are seated opposite each other.

Four players obviously play from all four arms of the board, which represent four districts of the town.

Each player has applied to the local newspaper for a delivery route, but only one is available. To find out who gets the job, each player races on his/her bicycle from the newspaper office at the center all around the streets and back to the newspaper office. Each applicant starts out in a different district.

1. Each player places his/her four markers in the corner on his/her left.

2. To determine who begins the game, each player throws the two dice. The player with the highest number opens the game. If two players win, they throw again.

3. The first player throws the two dice and moves his/her first marker out from the newspaper office along the center row nearest to him or her, as many spaces as pips thrown.

4. Players take turns at throwing the dice and moving their pieces along the streets. The path is in a clockwise direction, as shown by the arrows in the small drawing.

5. Observe these rules:

   (a) A throw of 12 entitles the player to an extra turn.

   (b) A marker landing on a block with a red traffic light (indicated by a circle) loses the next turn.

   (c) Two markers of the same color on one block stop the other player from passing.

6. How to win: The player whose four markers reach the newspaper office first is the winner.

To get into the newspaper office, a player needs an exact throw. In case of an overthrow, the marker is moved backward.

If a marker has reached any block on the center street of its district, a throw of 12 lands it right in the newspaper office, even if the marker is on the red light square.

Markers do not accumulate in the newspaper office, but are returned to the player's own corner.

VARIATIONS

Changed rules: The rules of the game can be varied in many ways, as long as all players are agreed on them before play starts.

More art work: To make the board more colorful, students can paint more designs around the basic stencils.

On the Way to School

To sharpen their powers of observation, have students look for repetitive patterns on the way to school. Once they are attuned to their search, they will discover unexpected instances of rhythmic refrains.

For the art period, two different activities are suggested. For the first one, which is more suitable for lower grades, students use their repetitive designs in a floor game. Middle graders imagine themselves to be graphic designers.

MATERIALS

Drawing paper
Colored pencils or crayons
Paper and pencil
Dice or a spinner

PREPARATION

The day before an art period, ask students to take along a piece of paper and a pencil and look for repetitive patterns on their way way from and to school. Give them a few ideas as to what to look for: bricks, bus windows, leaves, hedges, moldings, mailboxes in a row, grates, honeycombs, skyscrapers, flower petals, paving stones, tiles. Ask them to list about ten patterns and to make quick sketches of what they find.

PROJECT FOR LOWER GRADES

Students make drawings of what they have seen. Most patterns will be in a line, but students will be stimulated to vary their

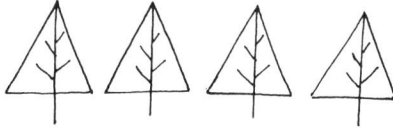

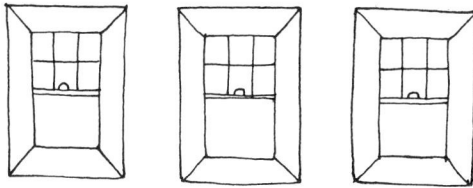

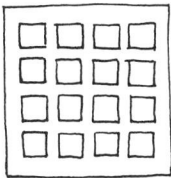

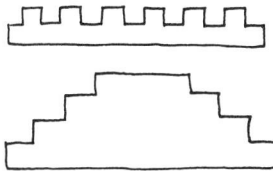

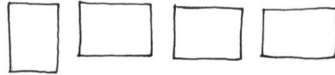

SCHOOL

play it again and again!

own work if you comment on someone's work that is a little unusual, such as petals in a circle, curlicues, or bricks that are offset.

HOW TO PLAY THE GAME

1. Students spread their drawings on the floor in a path. One end is "home" and the other end "school."
2. Each player has a marker in a different color.
3. The throw of the dice or the swing of a spinner shows how many spaces a player can advance.
4. The first person to complete the round trip from home to school and back home again is the winner.

VARIATIONS

Changed rules: Students can make different rules for the game, as long as they are agreed on before play begins.

Longer lasting game: To make the game last longer, obstacles can be created. For example, a player loses a turn at certain designated squares, or a player has to throw a six before being able to proceed.

PROJECT FOR MIDDLE GRADES

Ask students to incorporate the repetitive patterns they have observed into greeting cards. They can gear the cards to a specific holiday, if it is that time of the year.

Wild West

In making the board and markers for this game your students explore the art of paper cutting in two styles: geometric and realistic. The gameboard is made in the five-pointed star shape of a sheriff's badge. The markers are a horse and cowboys. The game is between unequal opponents: a horse and seven cowboys.

MATERIALS

Construction paper
Scissors
Glue
Pencil
Crayon or tempera paints

MAKING THE GAME BOARD

Each game board requires two pieces of construction paper, size 12" x 9" (30 x 22 cm), in different colors. One piece is folded and cut into a star and then glued onto the other piece for added strength. Practice cutting the star yourself, before instructing your students. It is important to have the paper in the exact position shown in the drawings.

1. Fold paper in half the short way.
2. Find the halfway mark on the side by bringing two edges together and indicating it with a small crease. Bring the opposite corner to the halfway mark and crease as shown by the dotted line and arrow.

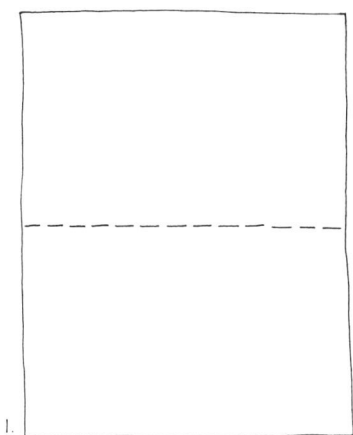

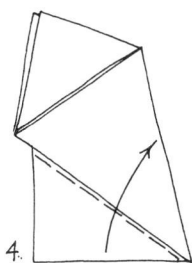

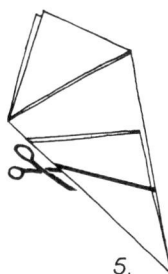

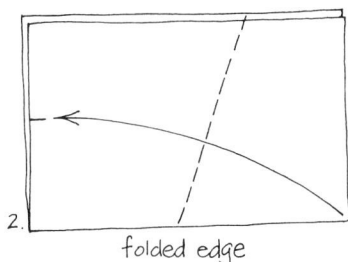

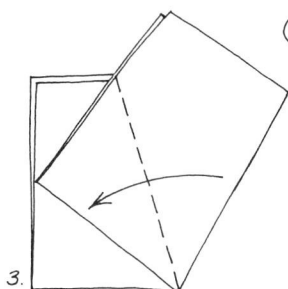

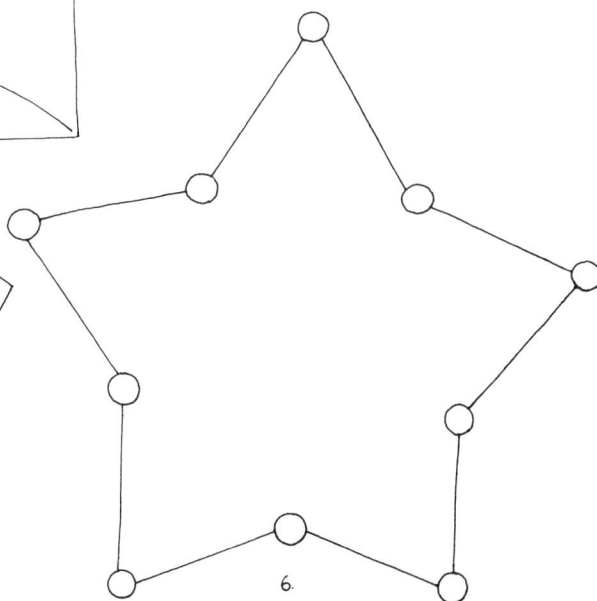

3. Fold the right edge over to the left and crease as shown by the dotted line and arrow.
4. Now fold the left edge over to the right and crease.
5. Cut as shown by the heavy line. Unfold ... and there it is!
6. Glue the star onto a piece of construction paper.
7. Mark the five outer and five inner points of the star with circles, which can be cut from paper or painted.

MAKING THE MARKERS

The game requires eight markers: seven cowboys and a runaway horse. They can be cut from the construction paper left over from the star cut-out. Students can exchange pieces to get a variety of colors.

The cowboy markers can be full figures or symbols, such as cowboy hats or stirrups. The markers can all be alike or different. The purpose is to give your students experience in cutting out and discovering that details are difficult, which means that figures should be kept simple. The stirrup shown in the illustration was cut from paper folded in half, which made it easy to cut a neat hole.

7 Cowboys

1 Horse

HOW TO PLAY THE GAME

One player is a runaway horse and the other player tries to capture it with seven cowboys. Players alternate turns.

1. A cowboy is placed on any circle on the board.
2. The horse is placed on any other circle.
3. Another cowboy is placed on a circle.
4. On his next turn the horse moves to an adjacent circle.
5. In turn all cowboys are placed on circles. For its turns the horse moves to an adjacent circle or jumps over a cowboy. The cowboy is then removed from the game. (He is injured by the horse.) When all cowboys are placed on the board in turn, one cowboy can move to an adjacent circle each turn, but does not jump.
6. The game is over if the cowboys trap the horse so that it cannot make a move. If the horse eliminates four cowboys, it wins, because three cowboys cannot cover the territory.

Grades 2-6

Go Fly a Kite

The art project for "Go Fly a Kite" is cutting, pasting, and designing with geometric shapes.

MATERIALS

Oaktag or posterboard, 12" x 18"
   (30 x 45 cm)
Colored art papers
Scissors
Crayons
Glue

HOW TO MAKE THE GAME BOARD

1. Give each student a piece of oaktag.
2. Explain that they are to cut a kite from colored paper and glue it to the top right-hand corner of the oaktag board. The most popular shape is probably the diamond, but some students may be familiar with the box, star or delta kites, and they can cut any one they like. They can draw the outline with crayon or pencil first, but cutting is different from drawing, so it is not necessary to cut exactly on the line.
3. Now explain that some kites have to have tails to make them fly better. (You may even want to discuss this in a scientific way, now or at another time. A book about kites would be helpful.) Tails are made from string or ribbon. Pieces of fabric or felt bows may be tied to them, and the more colorful these are the better they will show up in the sky.

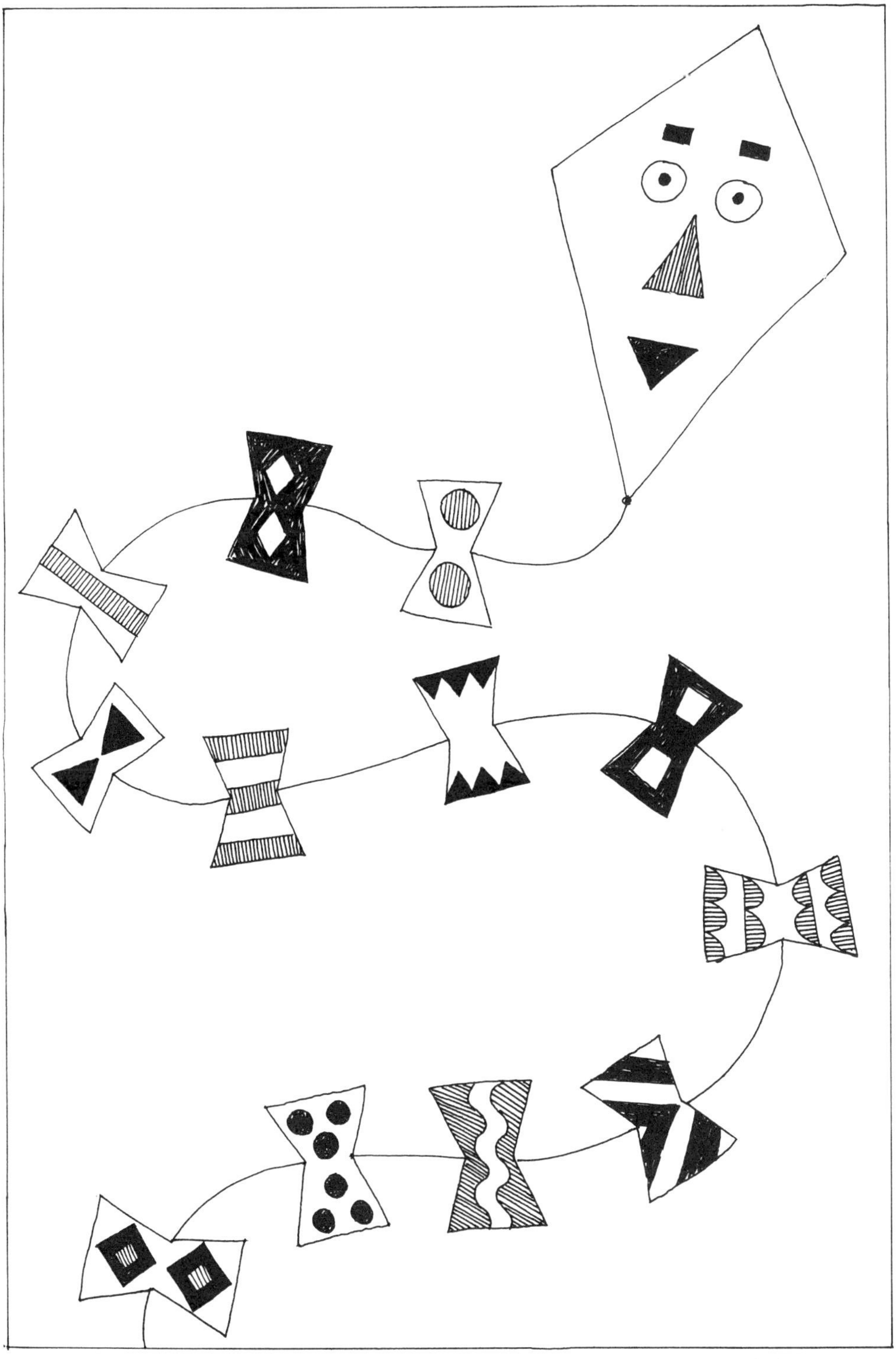

Ask students to draw the long string from the bottom of the kite. You can demonstrate on the blackboard.

4. From another piece of oaktag students now cut 2″ (5 cm) pieces which look like fabric bows fluttering in the wind. Once they have decided on a shape they are to cut 24 alike.

5. Now comes the fun of decorating the kite and the bows, which is actually an exercise in design. Ask students to cut out geometric shapes, such as triangles, strips, diamonds, etc., and glue them on. Make two sets of bows alike; in other words students make 12 different patterns in duplicate.

6. Glue one set of bows to the kite tail and use the other set as a card pile in the game.

HOW TO PLAY THE GAME

For two players:

1. For lower grades, each player in turn picks up a card from the pile and places it on the game board on the bow that matches it. For higher grades, the game becomes more interesting if three cards are removed from the stack. (No peeking.) They are then placed face down on any bow on the game board. (Still no peeking.)

2. The remaining pile is divided equally between the players. Each player places his stack in front of him/her, face down. The first player picks up a bow from his/her pile and matches it to the same design on the board. The player continues playing until he/she cannot match any space on the board and is eliminated.

3. The players take turns until one player disposes of all his cards and wins. If all spaces are filled up, yet all players have cards left, then the player who has the fewest cards is declared the winner.

VARIATIONS

Increasing challenge: Depending on grade level, students can make sets of more than 12 bows, which will make the game last longer.

Other designs: Instead of geometric decorations, students can make duplicate sets of letters, numbers, or spelling words.

Grades 3-6 for making
Grades 2-6 for playing

I Can Catch You Any Time

For this straightforward race game, construction paper is cut into a spiral path and then numbered. Players have markers representing animals, which they move along.

Spiral cutting gives you an opportunity to teach your students how to cut smooth curves. Tell them to hold the hand with the scissors STILL and move the hand holding the paper. They should practice this valuable trick whenever they cut paper.

MATERIALS

1 piece of construction paper,
    9" x 12" (22 x 30 cm)
1 piece of construction paper in a
    different color, 18" x 24"
    (45 x 60 cm)
Scissors
Colored pencils or felt-tip
    markers
Glue
Cube dice
Markers

HOW TO MAKE THE GAME BOARD

1. Place the point of the pencil in the center of the smaller piece of construction paper and draw ever-widening circles, about 1" (2.5 cm) apart, without taking the pencil off the paper. Cut on this line.

2. Starting at the outer end of the spiral, cut a strip ¼" (½ cm) wide away from the previous cut. This just makes a small space between the curves.

3. Paste the spiral on the larger piece of construction paper

Optional: Round and cut off the four corners of the spiral paper first.

4. Now ask your students to divide the path into 20 or 30 stops in the shape of stones and number them. Depending on the grade level you can suggest making fancy numbers, giving your students a feeling for lettering.

MARKERS

Choose any type of marker suggested in Chapter 10, but animals are particularly suitable.

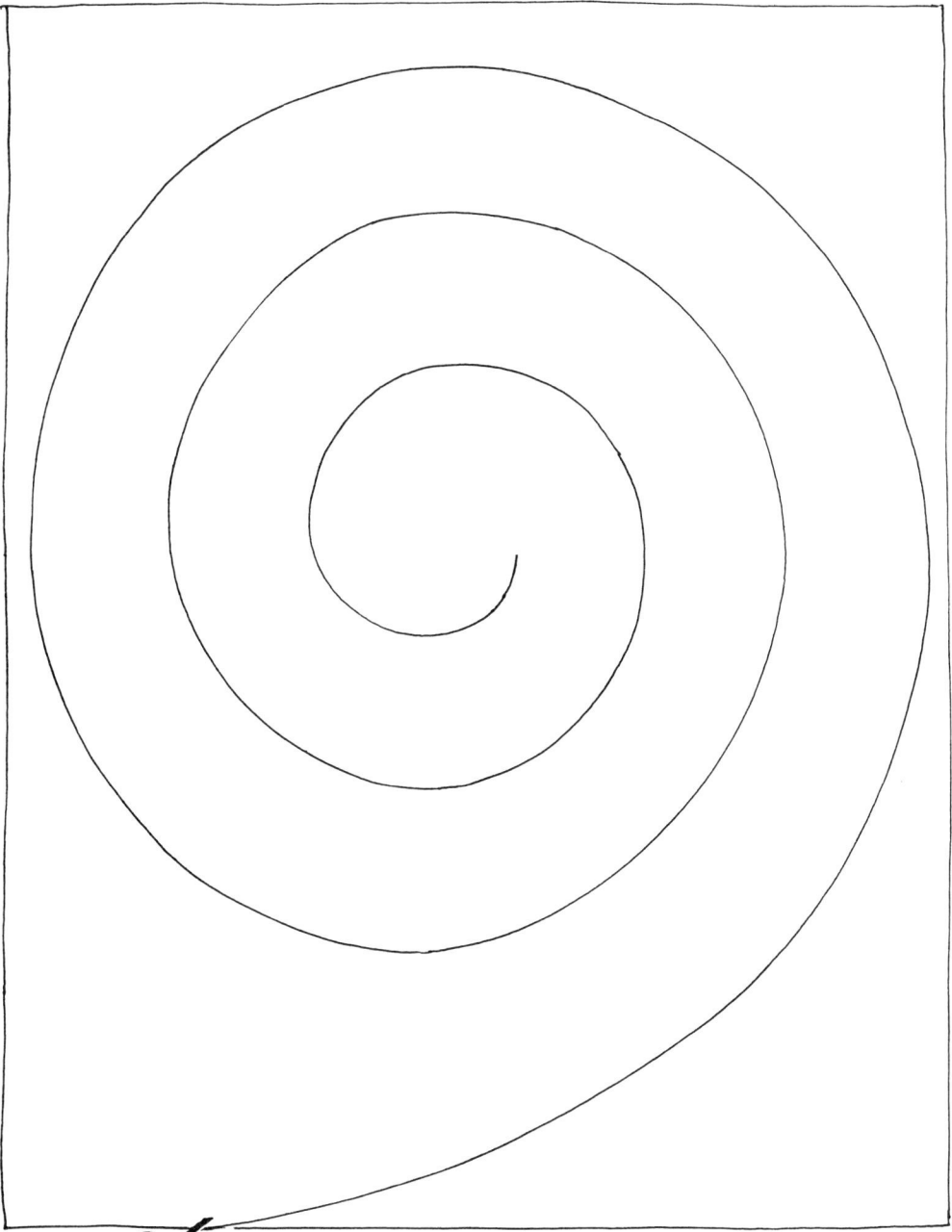

1st cut

HOW TO PLAY THE GAME

For 2-6 players:

The objective is to travel from the outer edge along the spiral and be the first to reach "Home" at the center.

1. The player who is to begin the game is selected by the highest throw of the dice. If two players throw the same number, they have to throw again.

2. The first player throws the dice and moves his marker as many spaces as indicated.

3. When a marker lands on a space already occupied, the player says: "I can catch you any time." The original marker is returned to the beginning of the game and has to start all over again.

4. To reach "Home" and win the game, a player must throw the exact number of pips. If he/she overthrows, the marker has to move back the extra spaces. On overthrows only, if a space is already occupied, then that marker is not sent back to the beginning.

VARIATIONS

Lower grades: Second graders can play this game, but need help in cutting the spiral.

Decorations: Decorate the "frame" left around the glued-on spiral with designs. You can set a theme which appeals to your class: snails, birds, monsters, clowns, fantastic creatures.

"The Tortoise and the Hare": "The Tortoise and the Hare" is a slightly more complex version of this game. Before the art period, get a copy of *Aesop's Fables* from the library and read the fable about the race between the tortoise and hare out loud to your class. Before students number the spiral path give each one six 2" (5 cm) paper circles and ask them to illustrate them with what the tortoise and the hare saw along the way: trees, grass, birds, houses, insects, other animals, clouds, people watching the race, etc. Let them invent a special place where the hare went to sleep. Glue the circles along the spiral paper path. In numbering the spiral, each illustrated circle is given a number. During play, whenever a marker lands on one of the circles, the player has to miss the next turn.

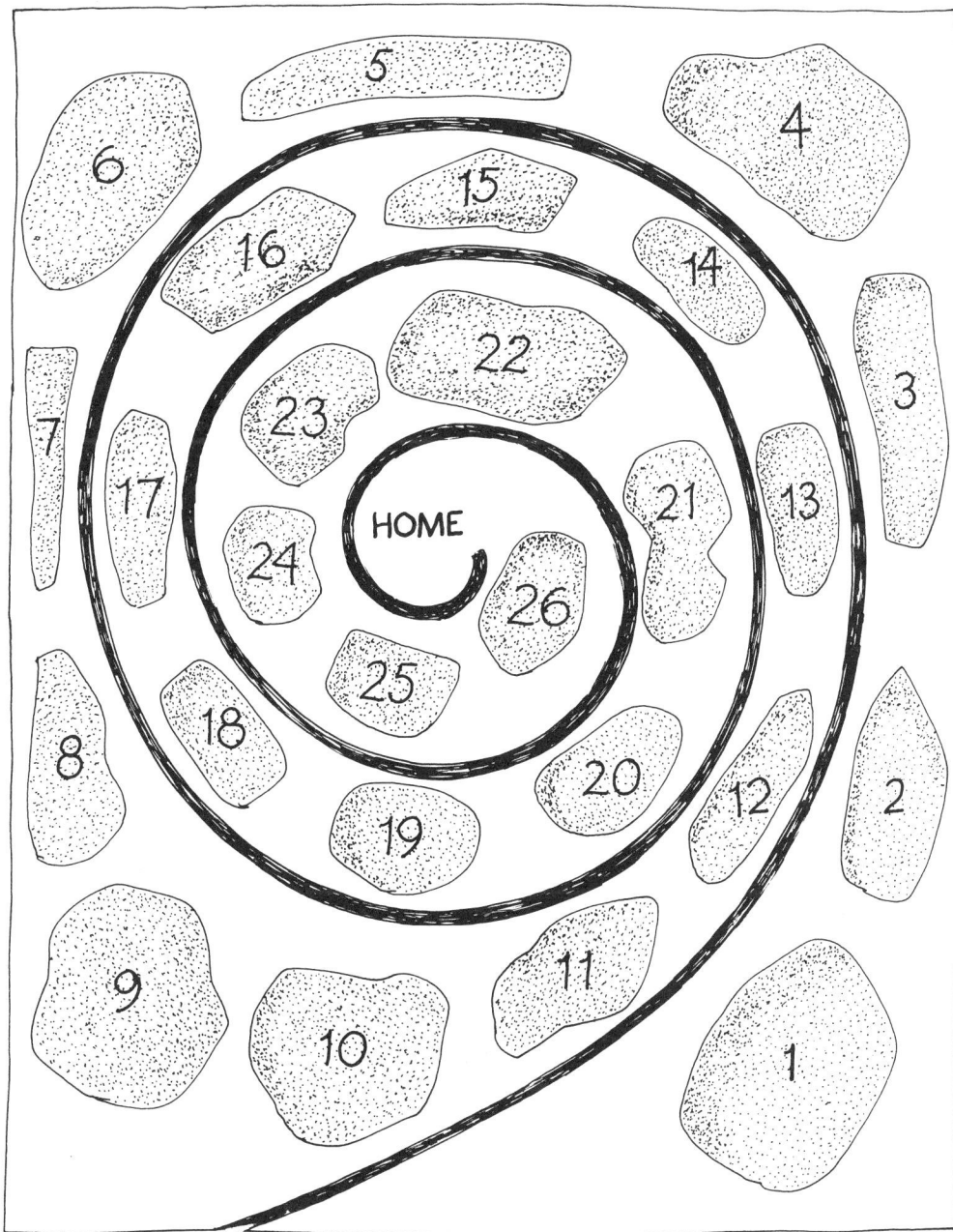

2nd cut

Checkers

Students weave a regular 64-square checkerboard with paper strips.

MATERIALS

2 pieces of construction paper, 12"
  x 9" (30 x 22 cm), in contrasting
  colors
Pencil
Ruler
Scissors
Glue or cellophane tape
24 markers (see Chapter 10)

MAKING THE GAME BOARD

1. Cut the two pieces of construction paper into 1" (2.5 cm) strips, lengthwise. Use either ruler, pencil and scissors, or a papercutter.
2. Glue the ends of eight dark strips on a light-colored strip. Use glue or cellophane tape.
3. Weave the eight light-colored strips in and out.
4. Glue the two layers of all the outer squares together. Cut off any extra lengths all around.

Optional: Glue the completed checkerboard onto a piece of construction paper.

1.

2.

play it again and again! 97

3.

4.

play it again and again!

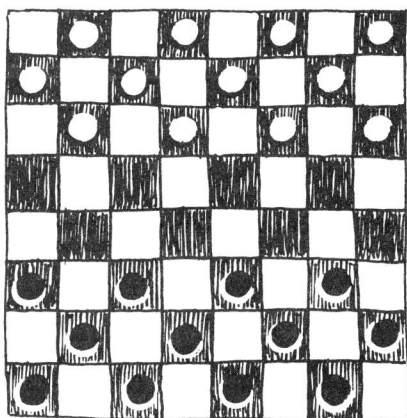

HOW TO PLAY THE GAME

Two players have 12 markers each in contrasting colors.

1. Arrange the markers on the darker squares, as shown.
2. Players take turns in moving their pieces forward diagonally one space at a time. Play takes place only on the darker squares.
3. An opponent's piece can be captured by jumping over it diagonally, if it is in the direct line and an empty square is directly ahead. The captured marker is removed from the board. It is possible to jump over two or more pieces if empty spaces are in between.
4. If a marker reaches the opposite end of the board from where it started, it is "crowned" by having another marker placed on top of it. This king is able to move forward as well as backward.
5. The game is over when one player cannot move any more.

VARIATIONS

Different sizes: Boards can be made larger or smaller.

Decorations: If the weaving is glued onto a much larger background, the edges can be decorated.

Art project: The checkerboard squares can be used as spaces for individual paintings instead of a game.

Other weavings: Paper weavings can be used for making placemats and greeting cards.

Konane

In this centuries-old Hawaiian game, markers always jump, which appeals to children. It is a larger version of checkers, consisting of a playing board of 10 x 10 squares. If your students enjoyed making the checkerboard, this project gives them more practice in weaving.

The Konane board can be made from paper all in one color, or in two colors.

MATERIALS

Construction paper or oaktag
Pencil
Ruler
Scissors
Glue or cellophane tape
2 pieces of construction paper in
    contrasting colors, for markers

MAKING THE GAMEBOARD

1. Cut 20 strips of construction paper 12" (30 cm) long and 1" (2.5 cm) wide, using scissors or a papercutter.
2. Glue the ends of ten strips onto a leftover strip of paper, to hold the weaving in place. Use glue or cellophane tape. (Is this the beginning of a hula skirt?)
3. Weave the other ten strips in and out.
4. Glue the two layers of all the outer squares together. Cut off any extra lengths all around.

Optional: Glue the weaving onto a larger piece of construction paper or oaktag. Decorate the borders with Hawaiian symbols: pineapples, palm trees, surfers, leis of orchids, shells, volcanoes, tropical birds, menehunes (the friendly little fantasy people of Hawaii).

MARKERS

A total of 100 markers is required, 50 for each player. Such a large number is most easily made by cutting small squares of construction paper. Select two colors that will show up well on the weaving.

Cut paper into ¾" (2 cm) squares. Opponents can choose different colors for their markers, or different shapes, or draw on two different, simple designs with felt-tip pens.

HOW TO PLAY THE GAME

For two players:

1. Each player chooses a marker design. Then all 100 markers are arranged in such a way as to cover the entire board, with opponents' markers alternating.

2. To determine which player begins the game, take one marker of each kind off the board. One player holds one marker hidden in each fist. The other player points to make a selection. If it is his/her own marker, he/she begins the game. Otherwise the opponent goes first. Put the two markers back on the board.

3. The first player picks one of his/her markers off the board, which must be either a corner piece or one of the two pieces in one of the four center squares.

4. The other player then takes one of his/her markers off a square right next to the vacant space.

5. Players continue with alternate moves, but now have to jump over an opponent's piece every time. Jumps are made to the right or left, front or back, but never diagonally. More than one piece can be jumped if there is an empty space after each hop and in exactly the same direction. A player is not required to jump over more than one marker at a time.

6. The game is over when one player cannot jump any more and thus loses the game. The game is also over if one player loses all his/her pieces, making the opponent the winner.

7. For the next game, players exchange colors.

VARIATIONS

Elimination tournament: Your class can have a tournament whereby winners of games play each other until there is a final winner.

Sets: Instead of playing individual games, a "set" can be arranged. At the beginning, decide how many games make up a set, which must be an uneven number.

Another version: In Hawaii this game is also played on a board containing 10 x 13 squares.

Chapter 1 2 3

Wall Games

4

7 6 5

8 9 10

Games that can decorate your walls

Button, Button

Children learn to match colors and practice addition by playing a tossing game. This project integrates art and math.

MATERIALS

5 pieces of construction paper in
    different colors, 6″ x 9″
    (15 x 22 cm)
2 paper or plastic cups
5 buttons, markers or pebbles
    (have extras on hand)
15 paste sticks
Stapler
Brass fasterners or cellophane
    tape
Cardboard or oaktag, approx-
    imately 18″ x 26″ (45 x 65 cm)
Paint or felt-tip pens

TEACHER PREPARATION

You have to make five pockets from construction paper and you can let children participate as much as possible.

1. Fold paper so that the bottom edge ends up about 1½" (4 cm) below the top edge. Form a pocket by pushing the sides of the top layer of paper and stapling into position as shown.

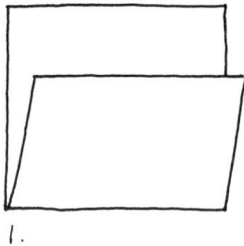

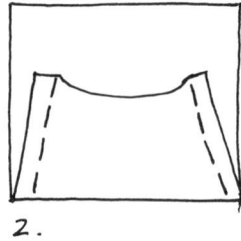

1.

2.

2. Number each pocket with felt-tip pen.
3. Attach pockets to the cardboard with brass fasteners or cellophane tape.
4. Attach the two paper cups to the lower part of the cardboard.
5. Paint paste sticks in colors to match the construction papers. Have at least three sticks of each color. Number sticks to correspond to the numbers on the pockets.
6. Fill one cup with buttons and the other with paste sticks.

HOW TO PLAY THE GAME

1. Children take turns at tossing five buttons into the paper pockets.
2. Each time a button lands in a pocket, the child takes a matching paste stick.
3. At the end of the turn, he/she adds up the numbers.

The game can be played non-competitively just for fun, or competitively, the child with the highest score being the winner.

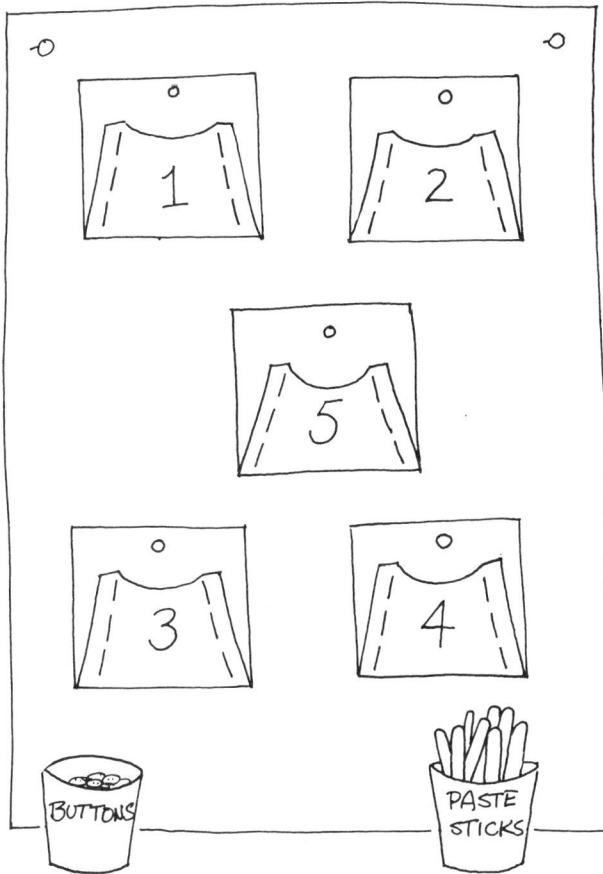

VARIATIONS

Higher numbers: You can increase the number of paper pockets and use higher numbers to make the game suitable for your class. Numbers need not be consecutive, i.e., you can use only even or odd numbers, or whatever you are working on in class.

Exact number toss: Play a game in which players have to toss one button into the #1 pocket, two into #2, etc. Make up some easy-to-follow rules.

Ghosts and Skeletons

This is a great project when Halloween comes around. You demonstrate how to make puppets from adding machine tape and then just let the class have a good time turning them into imaginary people. Set aside some time at the end of the period for judging the smallest, the scariest, the longest, the happiest, the silliest. Every puppet gets a silly title in the end and so everybody wins.

You need two or three rolls of adding machine tape which is sold in dime and stationery stores. Olympic-brand adding machines use a silvery tape that's quite spectacular. Used tape is okay to use. In addition, you need any kind of colored paper for decorating. Discarded magazines can provide a good selection.

MATERIALS

Adding machine tape
Scissors
Colored papers
Cellophane tape
Glue
Staplers

HOW TO MAKE THE PUPPETS

1. First explain to your class that the project is to make ghosts and skeletons from long strips of paper, and demonstrate how to make the bodies from adding machine tape. Cut off a piece of adding machine tape approximately 3' (m) long.

2. Roll it around two of your fingers. The unfinished roll should

have a center hole of about 1½″ (3½ cm). When the children do it, they'll have to wind the paper around three fingers.

3. Cut almost all the way through the roll in the middle, leaving enough to hold the roll together.

4. Bend the roll apart. It now looks like a pair of eyes.

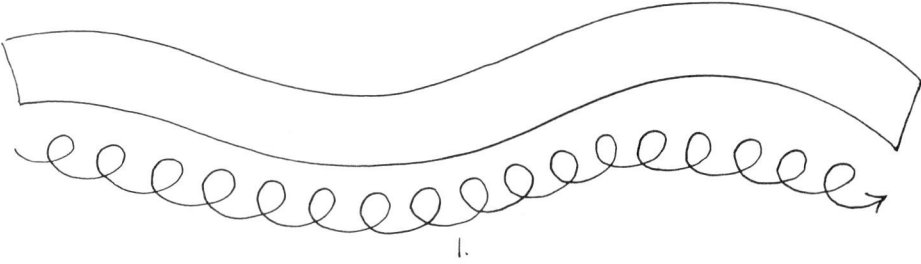

1.

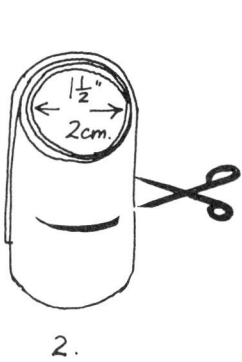

2.

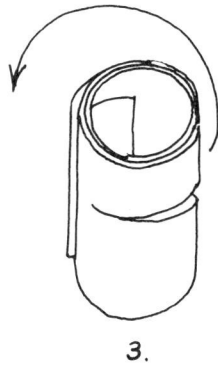

3.

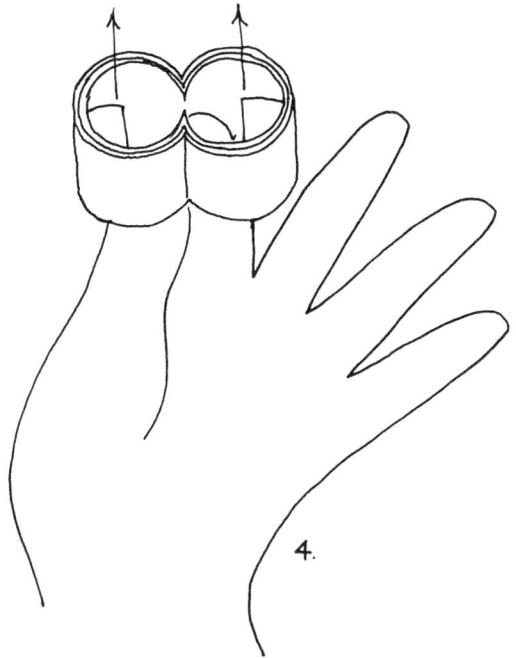

4.

5. Find the two ends of the paper inside and pull them out. As you do this, you get a long chain, and that's the body.

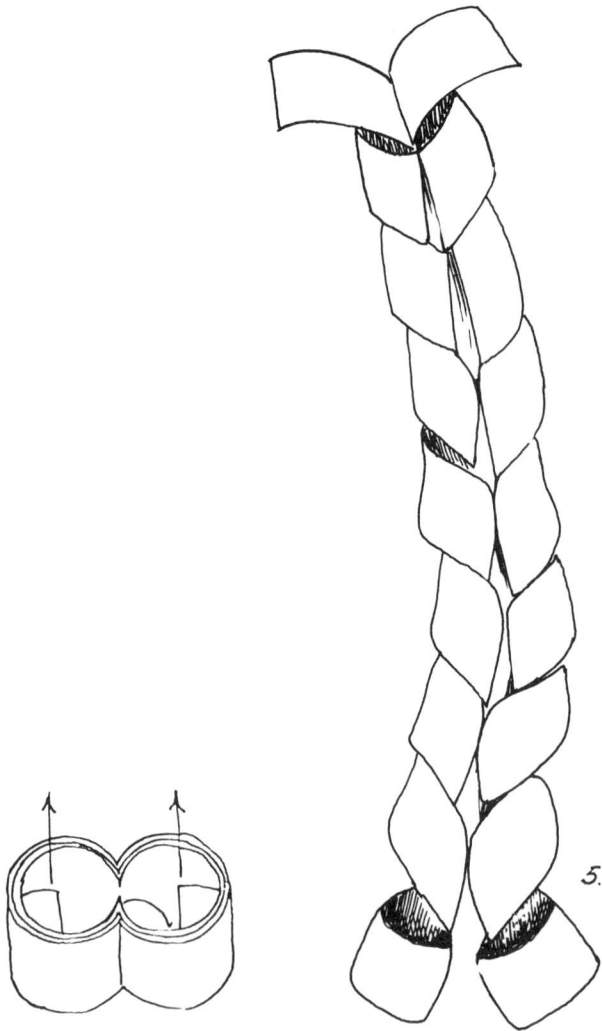

5.

6. Now distribute lengths of 3′ (1 m) adding machine tape to everybody to use in making these tricky bodies. They can be turned into people, animals, or fantasy creatures by adding heads, arms, legs, shoes and other attachments cut out of colored paper and glued or stapled to the bodies. Narrow strips can be cut from pages of magazines to be rolled and cut just like

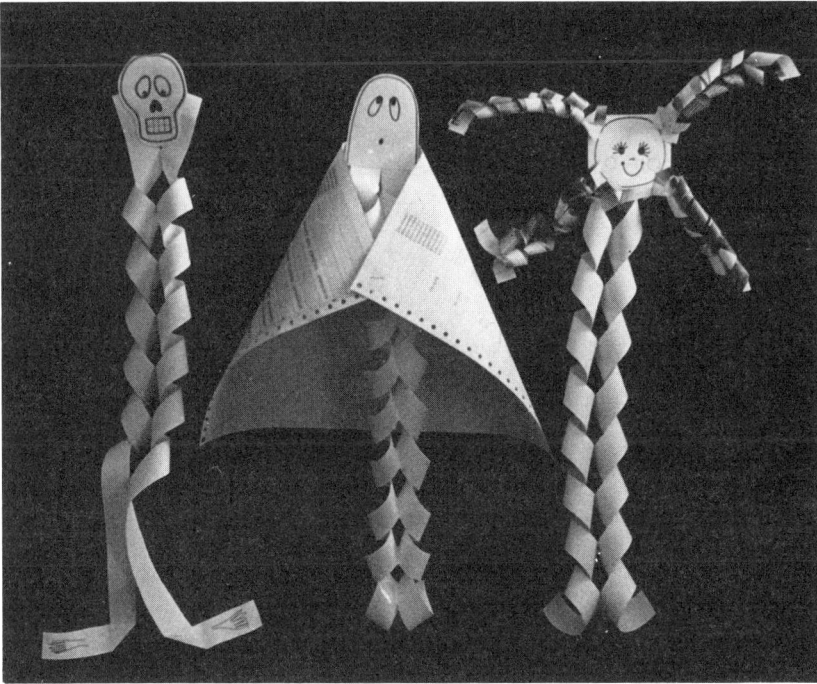

adding machine tape and used for hair, etc. When the puppets are finished, hold them by the top and they will seem to jump up and down.

THE FRIENDLY COMPETITION

1. Now comes the competition. With your class decide on ten categories to be judged: the longest, the smallest, the most original, the one that looks most like the principal, etc. Then have the judging. You can be the judge, or the class can draw lots for one of the students.

2. After the ten categories have been selected all the other puppets are also named and the class shouts out the title for the bluest, the most adorable, the sexiest, the baby, the one that looks like nothing at all, etc. Whoever shouts first gives the title.

VARIATION

Setting objectives: If you announce the competition before students make the puppets, they can work toward specific objectives to satisfy the various categories.

Raise the Banner!

In the tradition of the old-time friendship quilt, each student designs and sews appliqués onto a square of felt. The squares are combined into a banner representing the class. It can be displayed on the bulletin board, in the hall or exhibited at an art show. It can be loaned to the town offices, the local library, or other appropriate places.

This project introduces students to the idea of working with fabric and shows how separate units can be combined into a whole, while fostering group interaction. Arranging the squares into the final pleasing banner becomes a game.

If boys are reluctant to sew, point out that needlecrafts are now a unisex hobby. Some famous men, among them Rosey Grier, enjoy relaxing with needlework.

MATERIALS

1½ pieces of 9" x 12" (22.5 x 30 cm)
    felt per student
Scissors
Straight pins
Embroidery thread in several
    colors
Embroidery needles
Drawing paper cut into 9" (22.5
    cm) squares
Crayons
2 curtain rods
String or wire for hanging

TEACHER PREPARATION

Cut all felt pieces into 9" (22.5 cm) squares.

HOW TO DESIGN THE SQUARES

1. Let each student pick a felt square in the color of his/her choice.
2. Use the rest of the squares (and the 3" (7.5 cm) wide strips left over when you cut out the 9" squares) to make appliqués. Explain that students are to cut out pieces of felt from different colors and make pictures on their own felt squares. These pieces should not be too small, or they will be difficult to sew on later. Students can plan the designs on a paper square first, if they want to.
3. When they have arranged the pictures to their satisfaction they hold the pieces in position with straight pins. Then they sew them on close to the edge with a running stitch. You'll have to show them how to thread a needle, knot the thread, and then go up and down through the two layers of material.

Running Stitch

HOW TO ASSEMBLE THE BANNER

4. Place all the completed squares on the floor and arrange them in even rows, regardless of design. Then everybody together decides how to rearrange them so that the colors and designs are well balanced. If the banner becomes too large, you may want to make two smaller ones. If the number of completed squares cannot be arranged in even rows, ask for volunteers to make extra ones.

5. Join the squares with over-stitching.

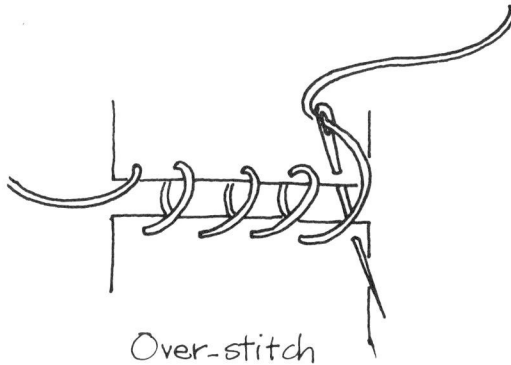

Over-stitch

6. Cut four pieces of felt 9″ x 6″ (22.5 x 15 cm) and fold them in half. Sew them to the top and bottom of the banner, at each of the corner pieces, thus forming loops. Slide the curtain rods through the loops. To make the banner hang evenly you may have to sew on additional loops to the remaining felt squares at the top and bottom edges.

7. Hang the banner with string or wire.

Chapter 1 2 3

How to Jiggle without a Saw! 4

7 6 5

8 9 10

Jigsaw puzzles and mazes

Grades 1-6

Hello, Pen Pal

Students make postcard size paintings, which they cut up and put into an envelope, ready to send to someone.

MATERIALS

Index cards, 4" x 6" (10 x 15 cm)
Paints and brushes
Pencils
Scissors
Envelopes

HOW TO MAKE THE PUZZLES

1. Select a suitable subject for making paintings on the cards.

Front

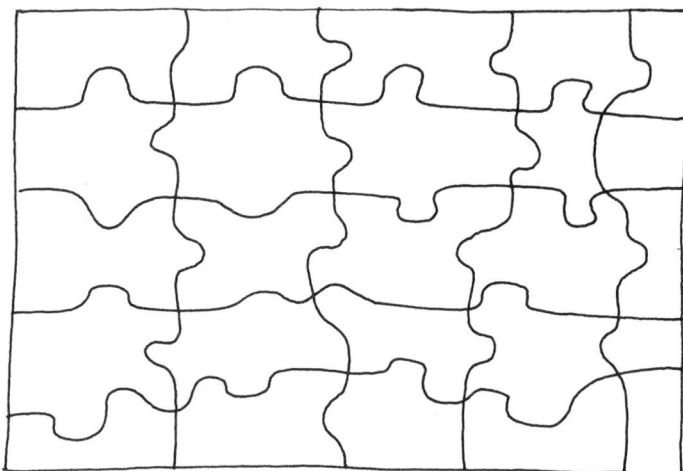

Back

2. When students have completed the paintings, let them turn the cards over and draw lines to outline puzzle pieces. Talk about what puzzle pieces usually look like. Why are they made with such curvy edges? What would happen if pieces were cut with straight edges? Note that the pattern is basically made up of four horizontal lines and four vertical lines with hooks.

3. Students cut the puzzle into pieces and put them into an envelope. Suggest they send them to someone they haven't seen in a long time.

VARIATIONS

Recipients: Send puzzle to grandparents, or as a Mother's or Father's Day greeting

Birthday puzzle: With wide felt-tip pen write "Happy Birthday to.." on the card, and then cut it up.

More difficult puzzles: By making the individual puzzle pieces smaller and in greater numbers, you make the puzzle more difficult.

Pen pals: If students would like to exchange letters with someone of the same age in this country or possibly in a foreign country, the following organization will help to arrange this:

Dear Pen Pal,
Big Blue Marble,
P.O. Box 4054,
Santa Barbara, CA, 93103

What's a Crocodile Doing in My Soup?

You have probably seen wooden puzzles that form an animal or a name, simple enough for a very young child to put together or for older children to display on a shelf. Let students make their own animal puzzles, but instead of wood have them use cardboard which is easier to handle in the classroom. You can explain that crafts people often design puzzles in cardboard first, so that they can make changes easily.

For this project students have to think about the basic shapes of the parts of an animal's body and the characteristics by which one animal differs from another. Displaying pictures of domestic or wild animals is helpful.

MATERIALS

Cardboard
Crayons and pencils
Scissors
Envelopes or plastic bags

HOW TO DESIGN THE PUZZLES

1. Tell the class they are going to make animal puzzles, and that each part of the body will form a separate piece of the puzzle. Discuss the parts of four-legged animals (body, head and legs). A horse and a dog have these same parts, but they look very different. In making the puzzle, the students are to bring out these features. They can color the pieces as they like.

2. Give each child an envelope or plastic bag in which to keep the puzzle pieces together.

Tail, down or up?

VARIATIONS

Riddles: To loosen up their imagination, let students make up jokes or riddles about animals. Here are three examples:

- What makes more noise than a pig at a farm? [Two pigs.]
- Why is a dog's tail like the center of a tree? [Because it's farthest from the bark.]
- What looks like a cat, feeds like a cat, slinks like a cat, but isn't a cat? [A kitten.]

Silly sayings: Let children make up their own sillies, which are even easier to think up than riddles. After all, "WHAT'S A CROCODILE DOING IN MY SOUP?"

Let's Visit Lincoln!

Youngsters who enjoy solving mazes are rewarded with a feeling of accomplishment, and that's to be encouraged. Rarely, though, have they thought about designing a maze themselves, unaware that this may be easier than solving one. As an introduction to maze making, show your class step by step how to construct "Let's Visit Lincoln."

This activity aids the development of visual perception.

Materials

Drawing paper
Pencils
Felt-tip pens
Erasers

ENTRANCE

Let's Visit Lincoln

128   how to jiggle without a saw!

HOW TO DESIGN A MAZE

1. Tell your students that any maze in a magazine or book is invented by a person who draws the lines on paper. The secret in designing a maze is to draw the through route first and then add all kinds of confusing dead ends.

2. To demonstrate, you can chalk a simple diagram on the board:
   (a) Draw a rectangle to outline a piece of paper.
   (b) At the bottom draw the entrance to the maze.
   (c) At the top draw Lincoln's log cabin.

3. Draw a tortuous path between these two points, as shown by the solid line.

4. With chalk in a different color, draw in misleading dead ends, shown here by broken lines. The tricky part is to make the forks in the road as smooth as possible.

5. Now let students draw their own mazes. Of course, they have to use the same color pencil for the through path and the dead ends.

6. When they have completed a satisfactory maze, they ink in the lines.

7. Then someone else tries to solve the maze with a pencil.

VARIATIONS

Complicating mazes: Once students understand the basic idea, they can build more and more complicated mazes, with longer paths and more dead ends.

About Designing All Kinds of Mazes

"Let's Visit Lincoln!" is a simple kind of maze to construct. You enter at one end and come out at the other. Here are some more features typical of mazes which you can suggest to your students. They are illustrated with fairly simple designs to bring out their essence, but it's easy enough to make them more and more complicated once the principles are understood.

1. The oldest known maze, which appeared on ancient Cretan coins, is shown in the drawing. It is usually referred to as a labyrinth. Similar patterns were used for hedge mazes in Europe, and the restoration of the town of Williamsburg in Virginia still maintains a walk-through maze of this type.

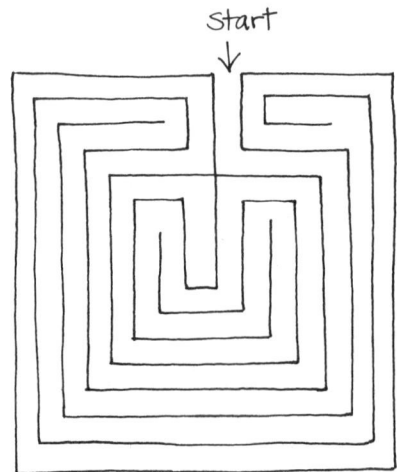

Cretan Maze

2. A maze can be entered at four different places, but only one path leads to the center. Follow the path of the waves in the "Sunken Treasure." A little more confusion is added by lines criss-crossing each other.

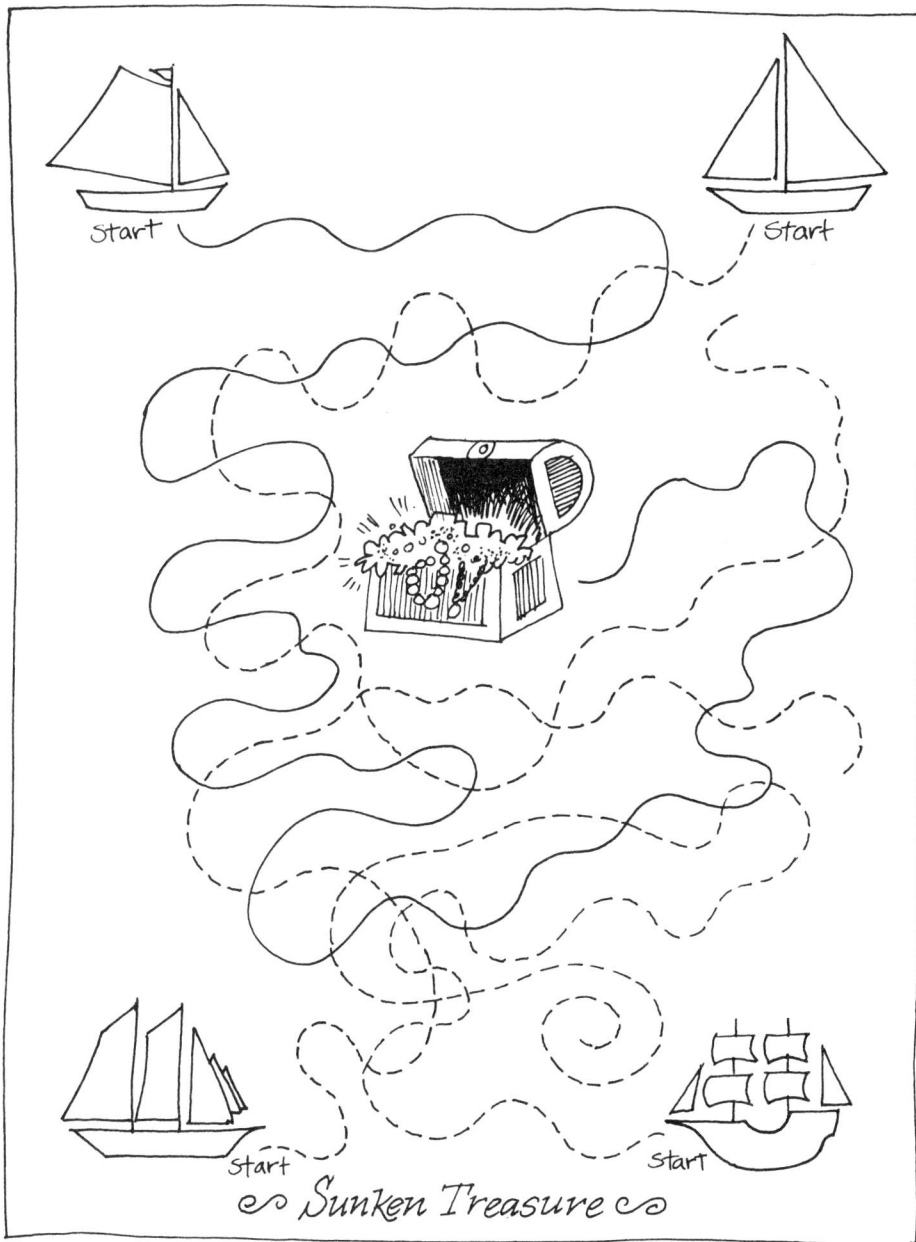

Start

Start

Start

Start

ᘒ *Sunken Treasure* ᘒ

3. The path proceeds on spaces between two lines, instead of on the line as in the Lincoln maze. "Strange Town" illustrates this method. The trick is to draw the forks with openings in two directions. This will become clear in the doing.

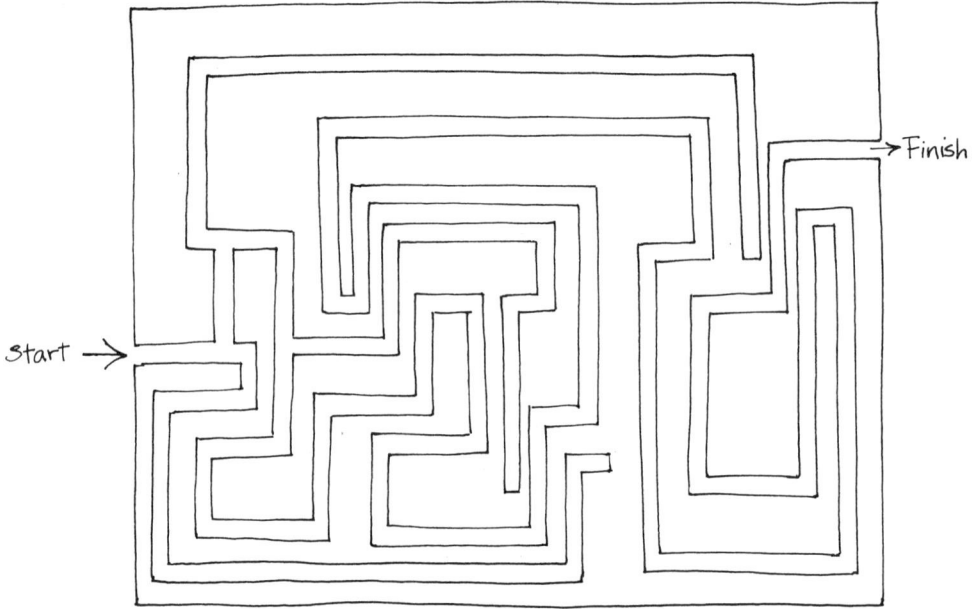

Strange Town
Maze

4. In "Football Pass" both beginning and end of the maze are deep inside the formation. A football-shaped outline is used instead of a rectangle.

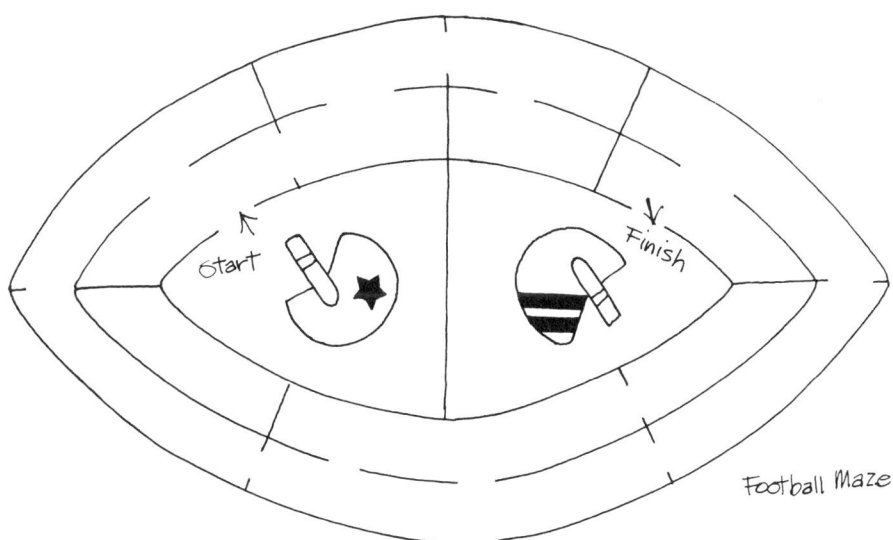

Football Maze

5. Coloring the empty areas on mazes provides a good art activity.

6. Some of your students may be absolutely fascinated with designing mazes, while others do not enjoy it. Afford the enthusiasts a chance to come up with novel ideas and let the others go on to other pursuits. Once interested students have done some experimentation they will get the idea that some of the variations can be combined. Published mazes can provide them with good sources of inspiration.

7. You can suggest titles for mazes to be designed, such as "At the Supermarket," "Finding a Lost Cat," "Travel across the United States," "Hansel and Gretel."

8. Any maze can be made semi-permanent by covering it with a piece of transparent Con-Tact® plastic or acetate. In this way a maze can be used over and over, by drawing with crayon and wiping off the lines with tissue.

Around and Around She Goes!

Building a maze on a box instead of on a flat piece of paper adds a totally new dimension—the third dimension, you might say. Your students should have designed some flat mazes before starting on this project. Ask them to bring in cardboard boxes. Gift boxes are easiest to work with, but many other kinds will do. If they have a lot of printing, they can be covered with paper in light colors, such as drawing paper or duplicating paper.

MATERIALS

Cardboard boxes
Pencils
Felt-tip pens
Optional: drawing paper,
    scissors, glue

HOW TO MAKE BOX MAZES

1. If the boxes do not have too much printing on them, they can be used as they are. Otherwise lightly glue plain-colored paper on the flat surfaces.

2. Design mazes very much the same way as suggested for the previous projects, but make the paths go over all six sides of the box. Entrance and exits can be on opposite sides, etc. The illustrations show paths made with flowers and birds' feet.

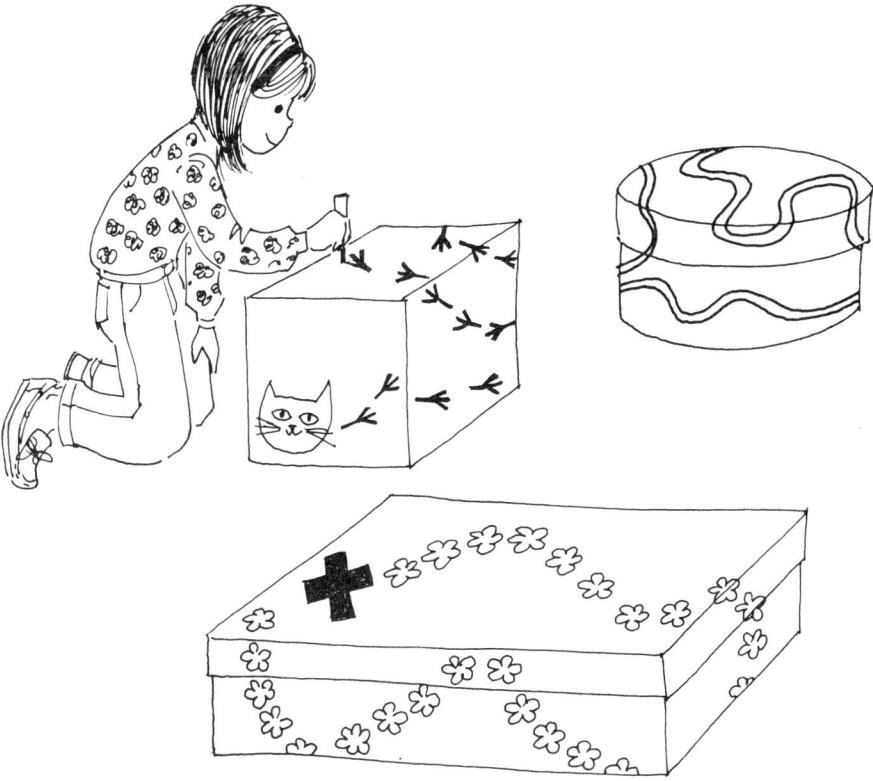

Mazes As Games

Mazes can be used as game boards to be played on by several people.

All players are armed with pencils and take turns in following the path. Any time a player reaches a dead end, the next person continues. Whoever reaches the goal first is the winner.

The maze game can also be played against time. Duplicate a copy for each player and distribute the sheets, blank side of the paper up. At the starting signal all players turn the paper over and trace the path. Whoever finishes first is the winner.

Circle Puzzle

Dissection puzzles are fun to construct and can keep a youngster (or adult for that matter) entertained for a long time. You may be familiar with tangrams which have been quite popular in school magazines and books. Here is a similar puzzle to intrigue your students and sharpen their wits. A circle is cut into ten pieces which are to be rearranged into figures or attractive designs. Students who possess an introductory knowledge of geometry can construct their own puzzles, but for others you should duplicate the full-size drawing and give a copy to each child for cutting out.

MATERIALS

Construction paper
Scissors
Compass
Ruler

HOW TO MAKE THE PUZZLE PIECES

1. Draw a 4″ (10 cm) diameter circle on a piece of construction paper.
2. Draw a diameter and another one at right angles to it. Both lines go through the center point of the circle.
3. On one diameter mark the middle points between the center and the circumference (here both marked with X's). The distance is 1″ (2.5 cm).
4. Draw a diamond as shown, connecting the 2 X's and to the points where the diameter touches the circumference, marked with Y's.
5. Now draw a line through one of the X's, parallel to line Y-Y.
6. Carefully cut on all the drawn lines. Cut one of the diameters first. There will be ten pieces.

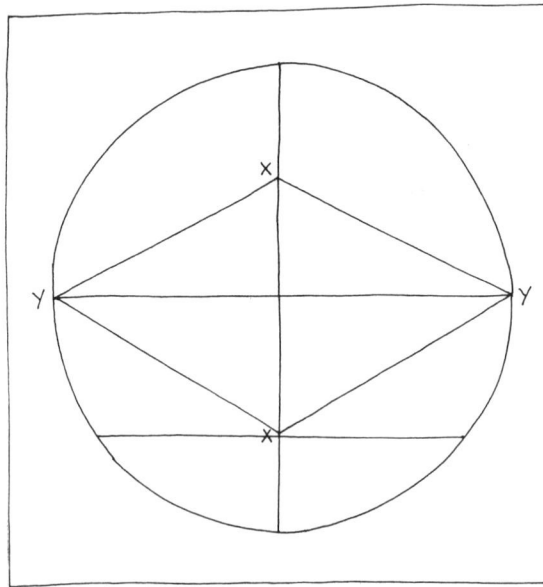

HOW TO DO THE PUZZLE

Rearrange the ten pieces into forms and figures. The pieces may be turned over. Four figures are shown indicating how each piece is placed. Two more figures are shown whole; after trying to duplicate them, you can find solutions on page 140.

One person can play alone or two people can challenge each other to make a specific form.

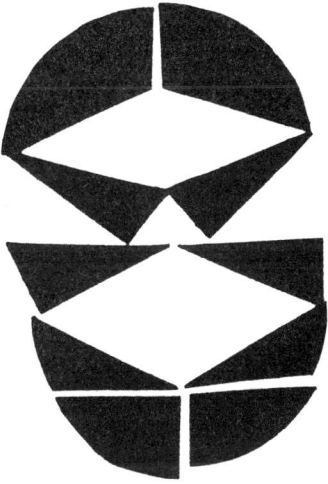

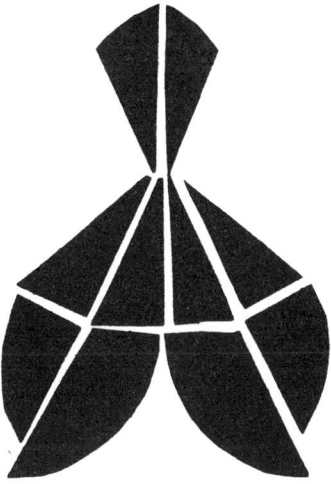

VARIATIONS

Reconstruction: Rearranging the ten pieces into the original circle is also a challenge.

Portable puzzle: Constructing the puzzle from posterboard makes it more substantial. Place the pieces in a plastic bag and bring them out to be played with at any time.

SOLUTIONS

Chapter 1 2 3

You Got Me!

4

7 6 5

8 9 10

Puzzles and games of skill

ABOUT PUZZLEMAKING

Most puzzles have to be constructed quite precisely, in contrast to games which leave a lot of room for working freely. Helping to release creative abilities in your students is one of the most important aspects of the art period, but there is also a place for competent handling of materials, which can be achieved with puzzles. Judge for yourself whether you want to present puzzlemaking as a free-time activity for individual students or get the whole class involved.

Quickie Star Puzzle

How can you make a perfect five-pointed star in a hurry? Knot a strip of paper!

MATERIALS

Lightweight paper, such as
   onionskin or tracing paper
Scissors

HOW TO MAKE THE STAR

1. Cut a strip of paper, let's say ¾" (2 cm) by about 10" (30 cm).

2. Tie it into a knot.

3. Hold it up to the light and what do you see? A five-pointed star.

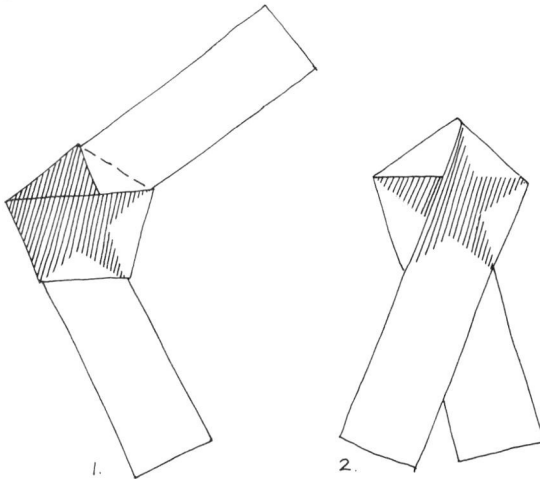

Optional: You will see that one line of the star does not show up very clearly. If you find this objectionable, you can easily outline the star with pen or pencil.

USES

Markers: Make the knot from colored paper and cut off the ends. This leaves a pentagon, which can be used for markers for some of the games in the book.

Christmas ornaments: Make strip stars with tracing paper. Cut off the ends, leaving a pentagon. With a little dab of glue in the center, glue the pentagon to a piece of colored tissue paper. Stick to a window or a lampshade with invisible cellophane tape. The light will shine through and bring out the star.

Cut a frame from colored paper and glue it to the edge of the tissue paper. In this way you can create tree ornaments in all kinds of shapes.

Jump This Way and That

In this age-old puzzle five squares in graduated sizes are to be shifted from one pole to another, moving only one piece at the time and never covering a smaller piece with a larger one.

It can be constructed from balsa wood, if available; otherwise use cardboard. Pencil stubs or dowel sticks can be used for the poles.

MATERIALS

Corrugated cardboard
Scissors
3 pencil stubs
White glue
Ruler

HOW TO CONSTRUCT THE PUZZLE

1. Cut cardboard into pieces in these sizes:

   For the board:
   2 pieces 12" x 4" (30 x 10 cm)

   For the moving pieces:
   1 piece 3½" (9 cm) square
   1 piece 3" (8 cm) square
   1 piece 2½" (7 cm) square
   1 piece 2" (6 cm) square
   1 piece 1½" (5 cm) square

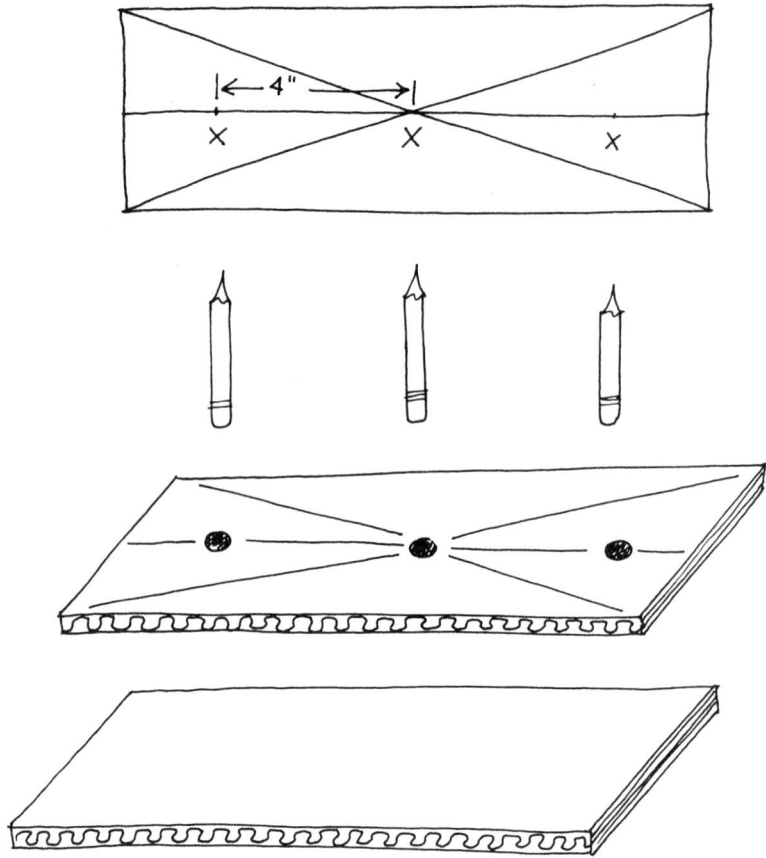

2. To find out where to put the three poles, draw the two diagonals on one of the larger pieces of cardboard. Mark with an X where they cross. Draw a long center line, and mark two X's 4" (10 cm) toward the outer edges.

3. With the sharp point of the scissors pierce the cardboard at the three X's. Then push the pencil stubs into the holes. You may have to slice off the rounded part of the eraser first.

4. Glue the two large pieces of cardboard together. Dribble some glue around the pencils to secure them firmly in the cardboard.

5. Draw diagonals on the five cardboard squares and pierce holes in the centers with the sharp points of the scissors. Then enlarge them by turning the closed scissor blades around in the holes until they are about ½" (1 cm), big enough to go over the pencils easily. Snip off any ragged bits around the holes.

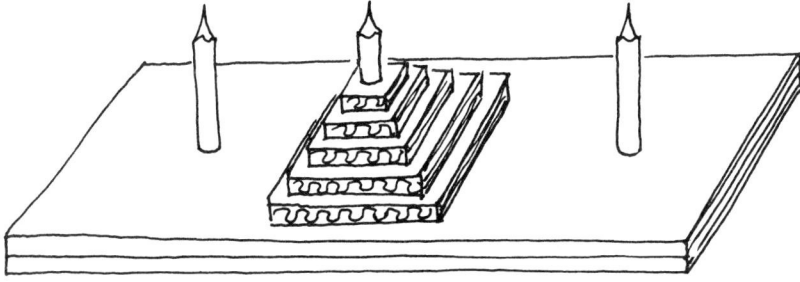

THE CHALLENGE

Place all five squares on the center pole, with the largest one at the bottom and the smallest one at the top.

The problem is to shift the pile of squares to one of the outside poles, one at a time, without ever covering a smaller piece by a larger one.

SOLUTION

The poles are designated X, Y, Z.

The squares are designated 1 through 5, beginning with the smallest.

At the beginning, all squares are piled on pole Y.

The moves to make are as follows:

1 to Z	1 to Y
2 to X	3 to Z
1 to Y	1 to Z
3 to Z	2 to X
1 to Y	1 to X
2 to Z	3 to Y
1 to Z	1 to Z
4 to X	2 to Y
1 to X	1 to Y
2 to Y	4 to Z
1 to Y	1 to Z
3 to X	3 to X
1 to Z	1 to X
2 to X	3 to Z
1 to X	1 to Y
5 to Z	2 to Z
1 to Z	1 to Z
2 to Y	

VARIATIONS

Balsa wood: For balsa wood construction, a drill is required to make the holes. For the poles, cut a ⅜" (1 cm) dowel stick into 3" (8 cm) lengths.

Decorating: It's easy to decorate the puzzle with geometrics before the poles are positioned.

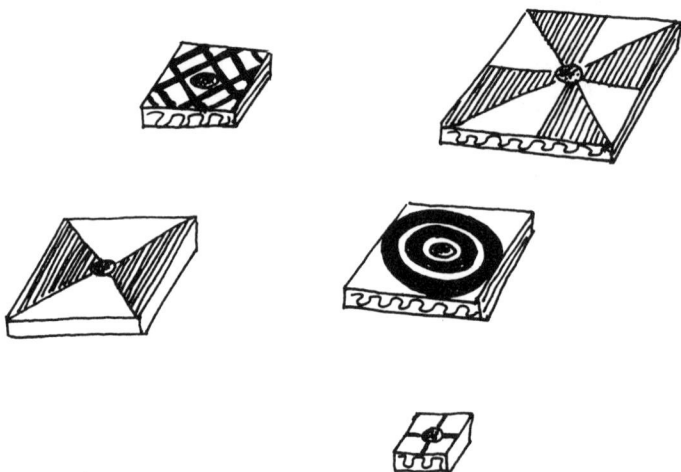

Grades 3-6

No Place to Go!

MATERIALS

A styrofoam meat tray
14 1½″ (4 cm) nails with large
    heads
A piece of tracing paper
Pencil
Ruler
Scissors

HOW TO MAKE THE PUZZLE BOARD

1. First make a paper pattern of an equilateral triangle. You can trace the drawing, including the small marks. Then cut out the triangle.
2. Have styrofoam tray bottom side up and place pattern on it.
3. Make holes on the three edges as shown, by pushing a nail through the pattern and the styrofoam tray.
   Then make three more holes in the center for a total of 15.
4. Discard the pattern.

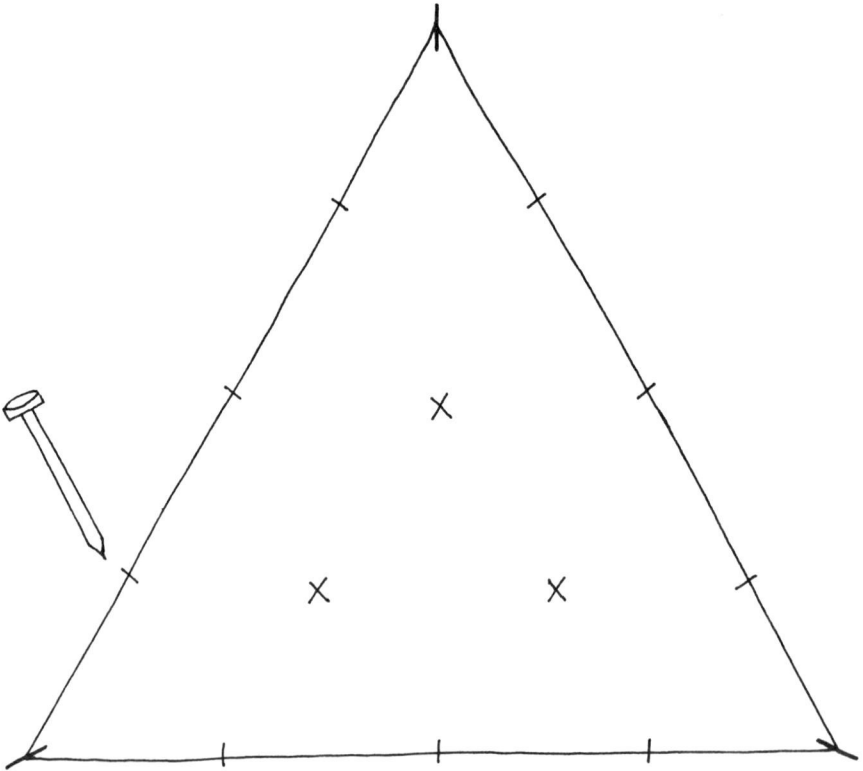

THE CHALLENGE

5. Place 14 nails in the holes, leaving one center hole empty.

6. Now jump one nail over another and remove the jumped-over nail from the board.

7. Continue to jump over one nail at at time, aiming to have only one nail left on the board at the end. On the first try, five nails may be left, but after a few tries the number will be reduced.

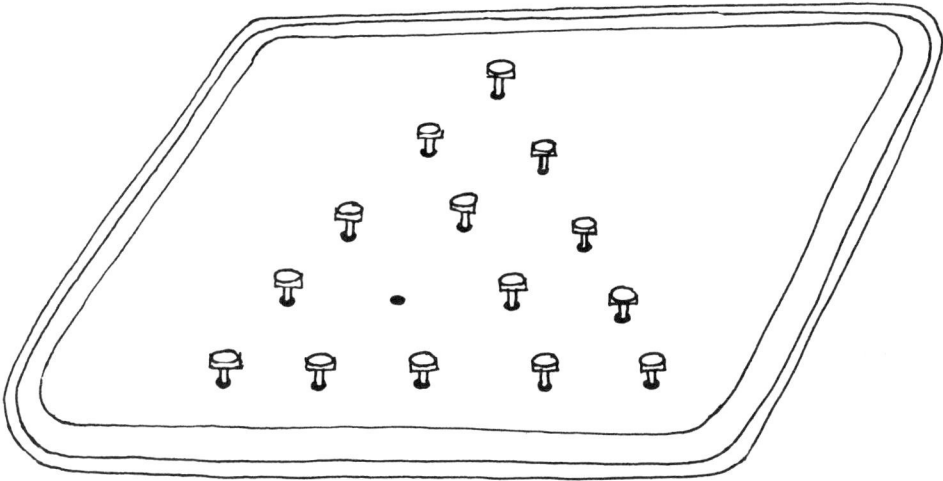

VARIATIONS

Golf tees: Golf tees can be substituted for the nails.

Wooden board: If you have woodworking facilities at your school, let students make the puzzle from wood, drilling the 15 holes. Pieces of dowel sticks can be used for markers.

Other games: Paint the nail heads in different colors, say five in red, four in blue, three in white, two in orange, and one in yellow. Invent games with different rules. Different point values could be assigned to the various colors.

Grades 3-6

Vacation Time

Students plan a vacation in an imaginary country. After they have drawn the outline of the whole country, they divide it into about 15 to 25 states. The puzzle consists of coloring the different states, but adjacent states must never be in the same shade. Do not urge students to fill in the areas too neatly, unless that is their preference, as this has no artistic benefit.

MATERIALS

Drawing paper
Crayons or felt-tip pens

HOW TO PRESENT THE PUZZLE

Introduce the project as described in the opening paragraph and emphasize that when the states are colored, the same colors must not touch each other. Let the students guess how few colors will be needed to achieve this. Now you can either give them the answer, which is four, or you can let them go ahead with the project and find out for themselves, which is more of a challenge for older students.

Mathematicians knew for a long time that only four colors are needed, but only recently, after long futile attempts, were they able to prove the four-color theorem mathematically.

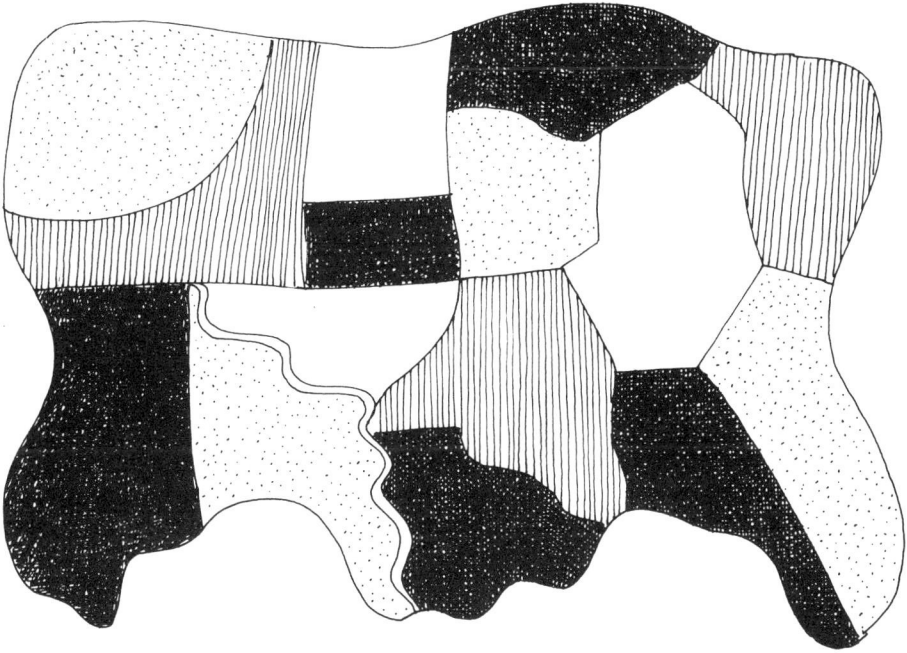

ENRICHMENT

Sightseeing: Have students make large maps and provide them with clay to model sights they might see on their vacation. Since they will be in an imaginary country they can include real and fantasy sights, such as mountains and rivers, the Capitol in Washington, D.C., the Golden Gate Bridge in San Francisco, cowboys, cactus, the Liberty Bell from Pennsylvania, Disneyworld (Mickey Mouse ears), as well as odd-shaped buildings and fantastic vegetation, animals, and vehicles.

Escape!

The construction of this puzzle is quite easy, but the solution takes a lot of moves, thus offering a special challenge to selected students.

The puzzle is made from cardboard, but construction paper will do.

MATERIALS

1 piece of cardboard, 5" x 4"
  (12.5 x 10 cm)
1 slightly larger piece of
  cardboard
A small piece of scrap paper
Scissors
Pencil
Wide felt-tip pen

PRESENTATION

Tell students that in this puzzle a policeman has surprised a gang of criminals in a warehouse, but he is trapped and trying to escape. Ten cardboard pieces represent the policeman and the criminals. You will show them just how to cut the cardboard.

HOW TO MAKE THE PUZZLE

1. Temporarily place the smaller piece of cardboard on the bigger piece and draw an outline around it with felt tip pen to form a frame.

2. With pencil draw a 1″ (2.5 cm) grid on the smaller piece of cardboard.
3. On the grid, outline the pieces with felt-tip pen as shown.
4. Then cut them out. Discard one piece as shown.
5. The large square is the policeman and the other pieces are the criminals. Draw a sheriff's badge or other distinguishing feature on the large square to represent the policeman.
6. Cut a small piece of scrap paper, draw a door on it, and glue it to the bottom of the frame.

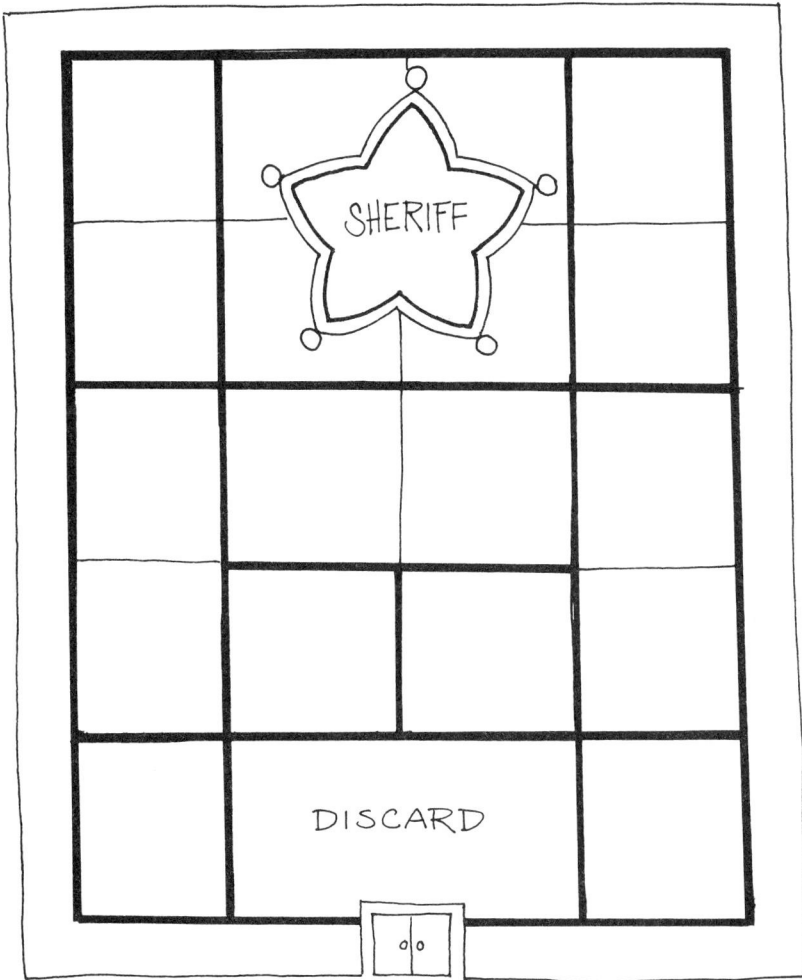

THE CHALLENGE

1. Place the ten pieces inside the frame.
2. To help the policeman escape through the door, shift the pieces around within the frame so that the large square ends up at the bottom instead of the top of the puzzle.

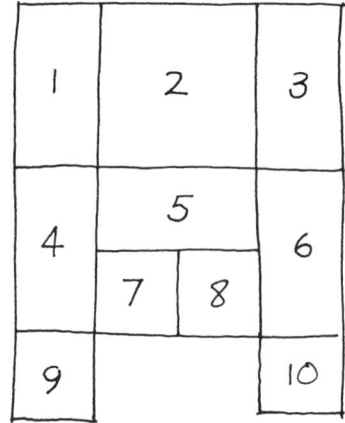

SOLUTION

For the sake of clarity the pieces are numbered, as shown in the drawing on the left.

Move 9 to right halfway,

4 down	2 down
5 left	9 left
8 down	7 up and left
6 left	8 and 6 up
10 up halfway	3 right
8 right	10 right and down
6 down	2 down
5 right	9 down and right
7 up and left	1 right
9 up	4 up
6 left	2 left
10 left and down	9 down
5 down	7 down halfway
9 right	8 left
7 right	6 up
4 and 6 up	3 up
10 and 8 left	10 right
5 down	9 down
7 down and right	2 right
6 and 4 right	4 down
1 down	1, 8, 7 and 6 left
2 left	3 up
3 left	2 right
9 up	7 and 8 down
7 up	1 right
6 right	4 up
3 down	7 left and up
2 right	5 up
1 up	9 and 10 left
4 left	2 down
8 up	8 and 7 right
10 right and up	5 up
5 left	10 up and left
3 and 6 down	2 left
8 right	

Chapter 7

Bet You Can't Guess

Games to develop imagination

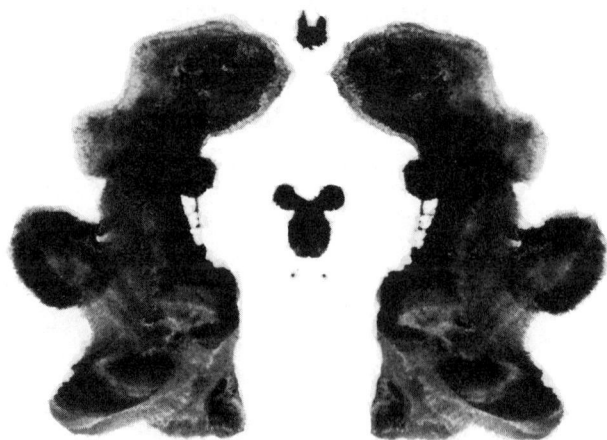

Feelies

"Feelies" heightens students' perception of textures and helps them in their art work.

For this game you place different things behind a board and have the students guess what they are. They can't see the things, they can only feel them. Are they birds' beaks, witches' feet, moon dust, or just stones and cornflakes?

In advance, collect many different kinds of things, such as rice, crushed eggshells, marbles, dried leaves, feathers, corrugated cardboard cut into small pieces, Silly Putty, prepared Jell-O, confetti, birdseed, sliced celery, grated carrots. Feel them yourself and choose things that are not easy to guess, bearing in mind the age level of the players.

MATERIALS

A grocery box
4 half-gallon empty milk
   containers
Felt-tip pen
Fabric to cover the front of the
   box
Textured things (see paragraph
   above)
Scissors and/or craft knife
Cellophane tape
Glue

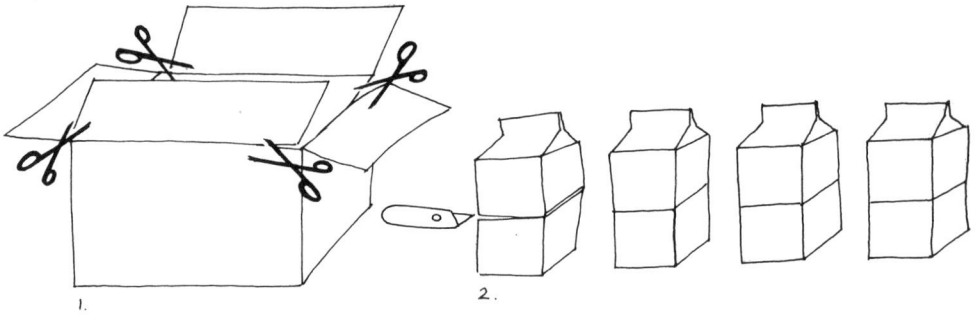

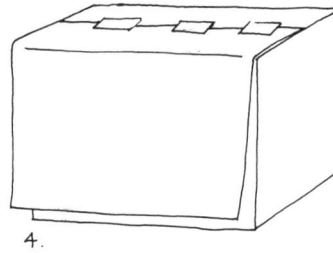

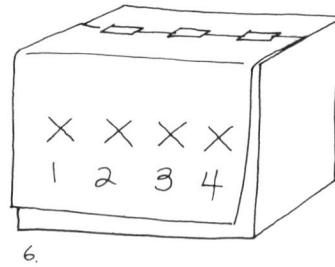

HOW TO PREPARE THE GAME

1. Cut away the lid flaps of the grocery box.
2. Cut off the tops of the milk containers, leaving them 4" (10 cm) high.
3. Stand grocery box on its side and glue the four containers inside. Above each container cut a square large enough to put a hand through.
4. Glue a piece of fabric over the whole front of the box (which was the bottom in its previous incarnation). Attach at the top and underneath with cellophane tape.

5. Reaching in from the back, cut a cross in the fabric where it shows through the holes.
6. On the front, draw numbers 1 to 4 below the crossed slits with felt-tip pen.
7. Fill the milk containers with "feelie" things.

HOW TO PLAY THE GAME

Each player in turn reaches inside all the numbered openings and says what he/she thinks is in there, and most important of all, what it feels like: slippery, prickly, grainy, velvety, rough.

VARIATIONS

More feelies: To make the game more fun, fix more than one grocery box.

For older kids: Let them write down their guesses and compare them later on. Be sure they are numbered.

Vocabulary: Each player has to contribute (orally) two descriptive words about each feelie.

Follow-up art project: Have students draw textures and also create different textures with paper by folding and cutting.

The Name of the Game

Most people do not know that designing letters is a skill. You can make a game out of making students aware that any letter can have many different faces. As examples can easily be found in print, prepare your class for the project by asking them beforehand to look at newspapers, magazines, and books to find different typefaces. The differences are most discernible in headlines and advertisements. Encourage students to cut out examples, but to make sure first that the newspapers and magazines are no longer needed. It is also helpful to borrow a catalog illustrating different typefaces from a local printer.

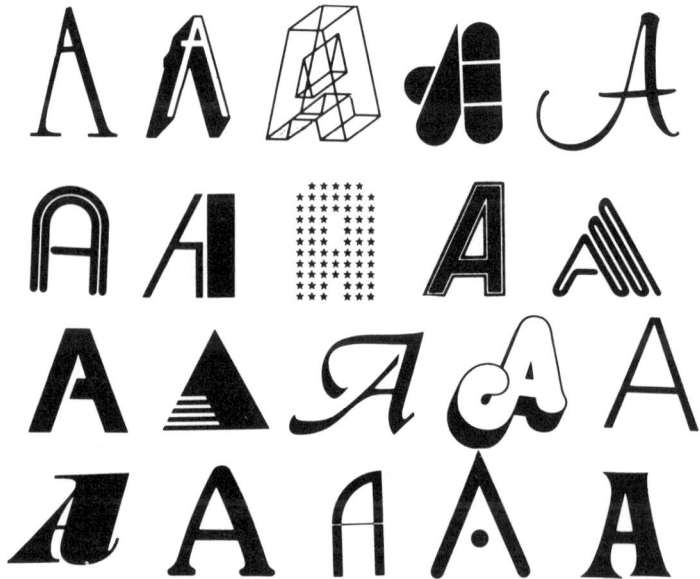

MATERIALS

Drawing paper
Felt-tip pens in different
   thicknesses
Scissors

HOW TO CREATE LETTERS

1. Instruct students to draw a letter, let's say A. Ask them to draw it large (about 4" (10 cm)) in two different ways: one as simple as possible and the other one decorated with several curls or hooks, keeping in mind the desired end result—an attractive overall design.

2. When everybody is finished discuss the different results. Are some A's easier to read than others? Why is one A more pleasing than another?

NAME DESIGNS

Now ask students to design all the letters for their own names, trying to have a uniform feeling throughout. If desired they can draw individual letters on small, separate pieces of paper to make it easier to redesign.

ART GAME

Students arrange letters in a close-fitting design, interlocking parts regardless of whether the letters are upside down or sideways.

Another person has to guess what the letters spell.

spells ROBOT

spells PIZZA

LOGOS

Here are some suggestions for types of logos that can be created.

Hartford Whaler's logo

VARIATIONS

Spelling game: Select the work executed by a student in "name designs," one that contains at least six letters. The rest of the class will be imitating the style, and you should therefore select work that you feel can be adapted easily.

Display the selected six-letter word and ask the class to write it down in their own handwriting. They will have a spelling bee in which they make words with only the letters in the name. For example:

Yolanda - and, land day
load, lay, loan

Christopher   stop, pot, her, spot, rise
post, port, trip, tip, this

As an added challenge, the students are to imitate the same type style as the selected work.

Competitive game: In the spelling game, whoever finds the greatest number of words wins; or whoever finds the most words in a specified period of time wins.

Design competition: At the completion of "name designs" or "art game," let the class select the person who created the best design. In order to be instructive, discuss with the class why some designs are better than others.

Cut-outs: Instead of drawing letters with felt-tip pens, the children can cut them out of colored paper.

Monsters and Butterflies

Unexpected monsters or beautiful butterflies may appear when blobs of paint are squashed on a folded piece of paper. A student's imagination is stimulated by guessing what they are. As an extension of this activity, let your students incorporate the blob figures into a larger picture. The accidental way in which the paint runs forces children to deal with shapes which they might otherwise not produce themselves.

MATERIALS

Drawing paper or newsprint
   paper
Tempera paints
Brushes

HOW TO MAKE THE BLOB FIGURES

1. Prepare several colors of tempera paints, making them quite liquid.
2. Demonstrate the project by folding a piece of drawing paper in half. Unfold it and place a blob of paint on the crease. Refold the paper. When it is opened a design appears.
3. Distribute paper to the class; advise care in not splashing the paint, and let the children proceed.

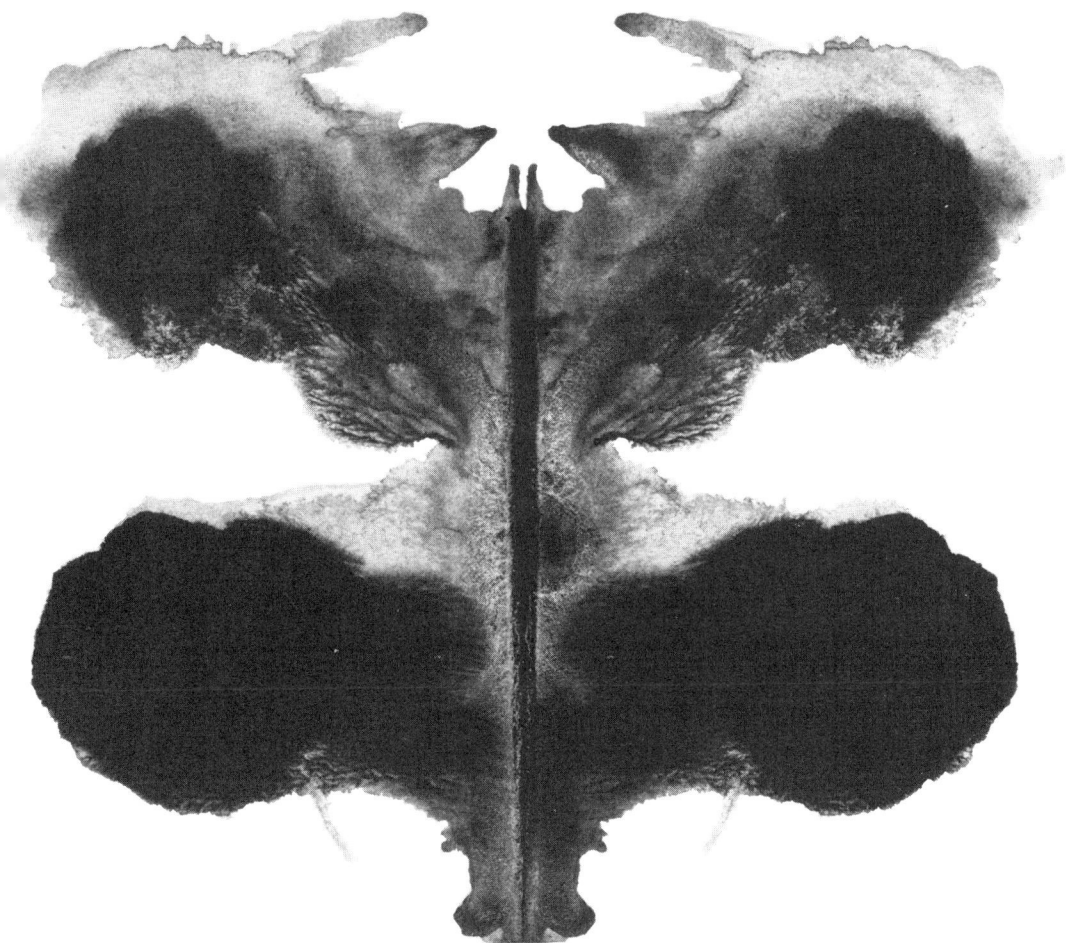

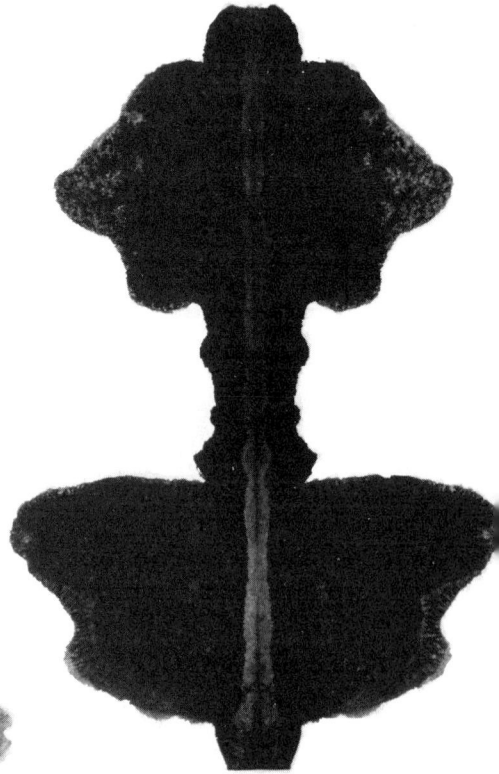

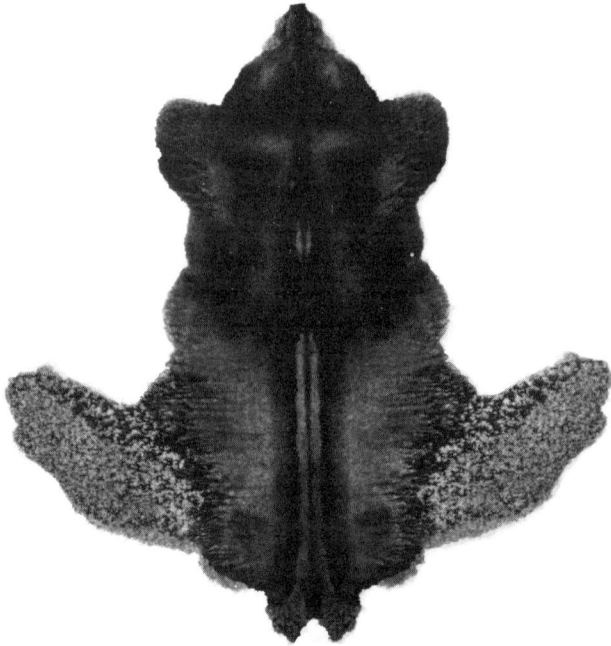

170　　bet you can't guess

GUESSING GAME

First you can let children describe what they see in their own blobs.

Then you can let the class take turns in naming what they see in other people's blobs.

VARIATIONS

Two-color blobs: Let your class experiment by placing two blobs in different colors side by side. What happens to the color when blobs overlap? Let this lead into a discussion of how colors are made up.

Blobs placed anywhere: Blobs can be placed anywhere on the paper, instead of on the crease.

Blob pictures: Students cut around blobs and incorporate them as parts for pictures. Added features can be drawn or painted in.

Grades 2-6

I'm a Cartoonist

In this game players ask their neighbors to do something, but the request is made by drawing, not by speaking. The skills being developed are quick sketching and communicating other than verbally. The idea of being a cartoonist relates the game to your students' everyday experiences.

This game is a good filler for a change of pace in your classroom, but is probably not suitable for a whole art period, unless you add other challenges.

MATERIALS

Index cards
Soft pencils

HOW TO INTRODUCE THE GAME

Tell students that today they are all professional cartoonists. Ask them to form pairs. Partners take turns in asking each other for something which can be either an object or an activity, but they will express themselves with drawings instead of words. For example, a drawing of a hand holding a pencil is a request to hand over a pencil. A person (even a stick figure) with one leg elevated represents asking one's partner to jump on one leg. A player is asked to arrange five books on a table, perhaps with the smallest book at one end and the largest book at the other end. Other requests may be to clap hands, or to stand in an unusual position. Cartoon style "balloons" with written words are not permitted.

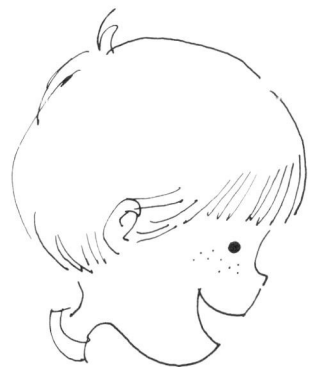

HOW TO PLAY THE GAME

Each student gets five index cards and takes turns in asking his/her partner to respond to a request. The drawings can be redrawn or changed altogether on both sides of the index card until the request is fulfilled. Then the other person takes a turn. If a partner cannot guess after three redrawings, he/she gives up.

VARIATIONS

Story: After the game you can extend the project by asking students to tell a story in four cartoon pictures. They will discover that cartooning looks very simple, but is not as easy as it looks.

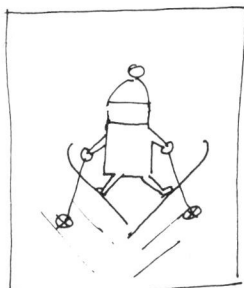

They will learn to eliminate details. You could discuss what is involved in drawing a cartoon story: you have to think ahead; it is possible to indicate agreement and disagreement between characters by the direction in which they face, etc. Ask students to analyze cartoon strips and see how artists show clearly what is going on. Could students invent a story for "Andy Capp" illustrations, disregarding the existing words? Do the words or the pictures tell the story? Is it a combination? Could you tell what is happening in "Charlie Brown" without words?

Colored cartoons: Students can use crayons, colored pencils and tempera paints, whatever is available.

Felt-tip pens: Ask students to think and form a picture in their minds for two whole minutes before putting pen to paper.

Team game: Divide the class into two groups. Each student gets one index card. One member of each team starts off with a drawing which the next person must guess. He/she then draws a picture for the next in line. The one who drew the first picture is the last one to guess. The team that finishes first is the winner. This game can be played with your class sitting at their desks or sitting in a circle.

Grades 3-6

Movies and TV Shows

For this game students create sculptures to depict a title or character of a movie or TV show. The completed sculptures are displayed and form the subject of a guessing game.

You should announce this project in advance, and ask students to bring in scrap materials. For more details see "teacher preparation" below. Allot more than one art period for this project, if possible.

MATERIALS

Boxes and other scrap materials
Glue
Scissors
Felt-tip pens, crayons, paints and
    brushes
Sticky tapes (cellophane and
    masking tape)

TEACHER PREPARATION

About a week in advance tell students that the next art project will be making sculptures of their favorite movie and TV shows, portraying either the titles or specific characters. They will need boxes in small and medium sizes (they can be collapsed for easy carrying), aluminum pie plates, used magazines, plastic containers, used giftwrap, aluminum foil, ribbons, string, plastic packing materials, yarn, shopping bags, cardboard tubes from paper products, plastic bottles, left-over self-stick plastic (Con-Tact®), sticks, tissue paper, etc. Encourage students to bring in as much as possible, as some of them will forget to bring in anything.

They should think about the sculpture they want to make and bring in specific materials, such as photographs cut out of magazines.

You bring in some grocery boxes in which to keep the materials as they arrive, and try to group the same kinds of things together.

THE PROJECT

Your students are not going to need much encouragement to go ahead with this project, as they will be full of ideas. However, they may find it helpful to know various ways to make stands for their figures:

a. Roll a piece of cardboard into a circle and attach the figure.

b. Take a box and anchor a stick to the center. Some stones may be needed for weight.

c. With the slit and slot method, two pieces of cardboard can be interlocked (see drawing).

d. Cut a piece of heavy paper into a semicircle and roll it into a cone. Glue or tape the straight edges together.

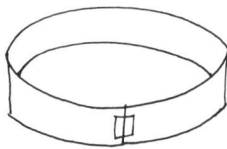

a.

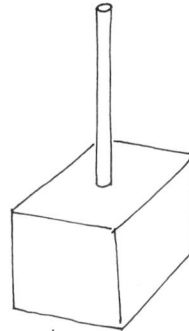

b.

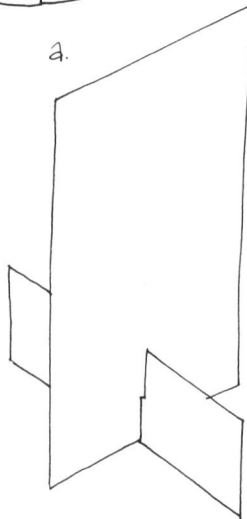

c.

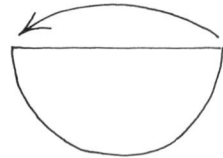

d.

THE GAME

1. Place the completed sculptures around the room or in any convenient area. Assign a number to each sculpture.

2. Arm students with paper and pencil and let them guess the movie and TV titles and characters represented by the sculptures. Whoever logs the most correct answers is the winner. He/she is excused from clean-up duty, maybe.

CLICK!

Chapter

1 **2** **3**

Let's Pretend

4

7 **6** **5**

8 **9** **10**

Games that encourage play-acting

Kings and Queens of the Past, Present, and Future

Fantasy enriches our lives, and in this game students make crowns to help them assume theatrical roles.

MATERIALS

Construction paper—18" x 24"
   (35 x 60 cm) is best
Scissors
Staplers
Glue
Crayons and/or felt-tip pens
Optional: oddments for decora-
   tions, such as buttons, dried
   beans, magazine illustrations,
   pieces of broken plastic.

HOW TO PRESENT THE GAME

1. Ask students to invent a story about a king or a queen, but keep it to themselves. Then ask them to make an appropriate crown from a sheet of construction paper. The many-colored, fall-off scraps are pooled and used for decorations. Give some examples of what the story could be about: a baseball king with a 450-batting average who suffers an injury; or a queen who reigns over a nebula millions of light years away. She is kind and hasn't

used her killing laser beam since she started ruling 39 million years ago. A revolt is planned. Can she avoid using the laser beam?

2. When the crowns are completed, students take turns in telling their story while wearing their hats.

The game can be completed in one period or spread over several periods, with a specified number of students telling their stories on different days. You should set a time limit of two to five minutes on the story-telling. Students can discuss the merits of other people's crowns, deciding whether or not they reinforce the personalities of the imaginary characters.

VARIATION

The game can be played in pairs, with two students working together.

K-Grade 6

The Great Train Robbery

The greatest train robbery in history took place in England, with robbers stealing the mail bags. For this project students imagine all kinds of objects which could have been in the mail bags and mold them out of non-hardening modeling clay, which can be used over and over again. The game is played before proceeding with the art work.

MATERIALS

Non-hardening clay
Toothpicks, sticks, forks, and
    other tools

PRESENTING THE GAME

1. Tell students about the train robbery. Some of them may have seen a film about it on television. Ask them what they think was in the mail bags, as all kinds of things are in packages taken to the post office. Toys, shirts, bicycle parts, Christmas gifts, money, whatever.

2. Later on each child is to specify one thing and the next person has to make it out of clay. As the game proceeds some of the suggestions may become quite outrageous, but almost anything can be indicated in clay. If necessary, you can ask a child to propose an alternative. If the suggestion is too broad, such as "Christmas gift," ask for a specific. This should take up only a few minutes of the art period, leaving at least 35 minutes for the clay work and clean-up.

CLAY WORK

3. Each student can have a lump of clay and make the object suggested previously. Encourage students to be as detailed as possible, using the available tools.

4. Exhibit the work in the classroom for a few days.

HELPFUL HINT

In Chapter 10 you will find some specific suggestions for handling clay, under "clay markers."

Birthday Party

Theater is an art form to be encouraged, and by having your students perform in class you can help them become comfortable in front of a group.

In this pretend birthday party, children act out what they would like to receive most of all for a birthday present. For example, you can demonstrate a bicycle by rotating both hands in the same direction. Stick out one index figure to connect the two hands; stick up the other index finger to indicate the front of the bicycle.

A new TV set is shaped by forming both thumbs and index fingers into a frame and placing them around your mouth, while speaking a jingle.

get that pepsi feeling

CLICK!

WOOF

One more idea: for a camera, one hand circles one eye and the index finger of the other hand goes click, click. Sound effects are permitted.

Not only hands but the whole body as well can be involved in this game, and your class will soon get into the spirit of taking turns, and letting others guess the nature of the birthday present.

Very young students tell about what they tried to perform, instead of having others guess.

As "Birthday Party" is such a valuable experience, you may want to play it at least once a month. Each month you could put the names of children who have birthdays in a bag and draw out one name. On that child's birth date, you play the game.

I Am Angry at You

This game lets children take turns in acting out some of their frustrations.

Each student pretends to be two people: him- or her-self and another person at whom to be angry. He/she then conducts an argument, changing positions and tone of voice, depending on who is speaking.

Johnny is having an argument with his mother. Johnny, speaking in his own voice: "I want to go over to Jimmy's house."

Johnny then turns his head and speaks, imitating his mother's voice: "It's too close to dinner time and besides, it's raining."

Johnny: "I promise I'll be right back."

Etc. etc.

You end the argument after a short while and let the next child have a turn. The class can talk about what happened, not necessarily saying that Johnny is right or wrong. Someone may say: "Yeah, my mother did the same to me last week." In this way children realize that these things also happen to their peers.

Mary might have an argument with her sister or a baby sitter or the school crossing guard. Avoid direct arguments between child and teacher.

It is best to play this game when you are a few weeks into the school year. By then you know your class and the students know each other.

K-Grade 6

I'm a Super-Star

In this game students imagine they have fantastic abilities and act them out. The child pretends to be a helicopter by flapping his/her arms and flies off to visit grandma and grandpa who live far away. Or the child runs in place furiously because he/she has invented a secret orange drink and as a result can now run faster than anyone. Or the child forms a magic circle with index finger and thumb, which heals any sore right away.

Depending on the space available, you can have the whole class or a small group acting as super-stars at the same time.

Afterwards let each child express in just a couple of sentences how it felt to be a super-star. "I thought I could do anything." "My grandma was surprised to see me." This comment does not express the child's own feelings, so you say: "But how did you feel when you saw your grandparents?" Then the child may say: "I was happy too." The magic circle may produce the comment: "I am going to be a doctor, because I want to help people."

Chapter 1 2 3 4 5 6 7 8 9 10

Leftovers

Games too good to be left out

FBI Agent

This training session for secret service agents will help your students train their memory and sharpen their powers of observation. Five items are on view for the count of ten, and are then covered up. Students have to remember how they were arranged.

MATERIALS

Pieces of construction paper,
   9″ x 12″ (22.5 x 30 cm)
One larger sheet of paper
Scissors
Ruler
Pen

TEACHER PREPARATION

1. Allow one sheet of construction paper per student, plus a few extra.
2. Cut the sheets into 9″ (22.5 cm) squares. Put the leftover strips in a pile.
3. Divide the papers into nine 3″ (7.5 cm) squares, using pen and ruler. Each paper will look like a board for tic-tac-toe.

   Older students can perform steps 2 and 3 themselves.

HOW TO PRESENT THE GAME

4. Give each student one of the 9-square playing boards.

5. Tell students that today they are all secret service agents in the FBI. They are undergoing a training session to prepare them to take in as many details as possible, as quickly as possible, when they arrive at the scene of a crime. First they are going to cut out five things found in the room where a crime took place.

HOW TO MAKE THE CUT-OUTS

6. Let each student select a strip of construction paper from the pile (choosing a different color than his/her playing board), then divide and cut the strip into five pieces.

7. Announce that the students are to cut out—

> a cup
> an apple
> a telephone
> a shoe and
> a dog.

cut out
shapes

Write the name of these five figures on the blackboard to help the children remember. Extra construction paper may come in handy as they may not be satisfied with their first effort at cutting out.

HOW TO PLAY THE GAME

1. Select one student to be the criminal, and have him/her sit in the middle of a circle of seated classmates. As an alternative, you can divide the class into several separate play groups.

2. The criminal places the five objects on the board in any arrangement, then covers the objects with the larger sheet of paper so that no one can see them. The paper is removed and the secret service agents are allowed to observe the evidence for the count

of ten. Then the sheet of paper is replaced. Now the FBI agents try to duplicate the arrangement on their own boards.

3. A full game consists of seven tries. Each correct "copy" made by an FBI agent scores one point. The winner is the agent with the most points at the end of seven rounds.

4. A new criminal is chosen for the next seven rounds.

VARIATIONS

Countdown: Adjust the countdown time as necessary. If everybody gets the arrangement by the count of ten, reduce the count. If nobody can manage very well, lengthen the countdown or use only three or four objects.

Other objects: You can of course substitute other things, or let the class decide what things the agents found in the room. One obvious item is left out on purpose: a gun—but that's up to you.

Two-person game: If only two kids play together, one being the criminal and the other an FBI agent, then the whole class does not have to cut out identical objects, but each child can decide on his/ her own cut-outs.

Color game: Make the boards from white paper and cut circles (or other shapes) from construction paper in five different colors. Each student has to end up with five circles in different colors. FBI agents have to remember the position of the colors.

Addition game: For lower grades adapt the game for math training. Chalk nine squares on the blackboard. Insert five numbers in any squares, using single or double digits, depending on grade levels.

Ask children to add up numbers crosswise and downward and write down the answers. After a specified countdown, erase the numbers. Whoever has all the correct answers wins.

Geometry enrichment: Substitute geometric forms for realistic objects by having students draw simple shapes on pieces of paper. Compass and ruler will help them draw equilateral triangles, semicircles, hexagons, or whatever you would like them to work on.

Other craft materials: Instead of paper cut-outs, select clay or any of the other suggestions given for making markers in Chapter 10.

Piles of Tiles

Most of your students are familiar with tiled kitchen floors and bathroom walls. Some tiles are in plain colors, but others have repeating patterns where the design of one tile flows into the next. Creating tile patterns is a fascinating activity, which is explored in two projects. The first employs only 16 tiles so that students can grasp the underlying principle. After that they can experiment in whatever direction they choose, producing unexpected surprises which are so much part of tiling. You might suggest that your students look closely at the patterns whenever they see tiles.

Although construction paper is specified, almost any kind of paper is suitable, depending on what you have available, varying from the least expensive type of duplicating paper to thin cardboard.

MATERIALS

For tiles: construction paper in
  light colors
For background: any color construction paper, 9" x 12"
  (22 x 30 cm)
Paper cutter (or pencil, ruler and
  scissors)
Paste or glue
Felt-tip pens or crayons

First project

TEACHER PREPARATION

Cut light-colored paper into 1½" (4 cm) squares. (An older student could do this.) Allow 16 squares per student.

CREATING TILE PATTERNS

1. Each student has 16 squares. Ask everyone to draw a design on one corner of a square. It can be as simple as a line across the corner, or a heart or a flower. Three examples are given, which you can draw on the board.

2. Ask students to repeat their designs on the corner of the other 15 squares, as nearly as possible in the same size.
3. Now ask them to arrange four squares with the four decorated corners touching.
4. Arrange the remaining 12 squares in exactly the same way and push all 16 squares together.
5. Glue the tiles onto the background paper.

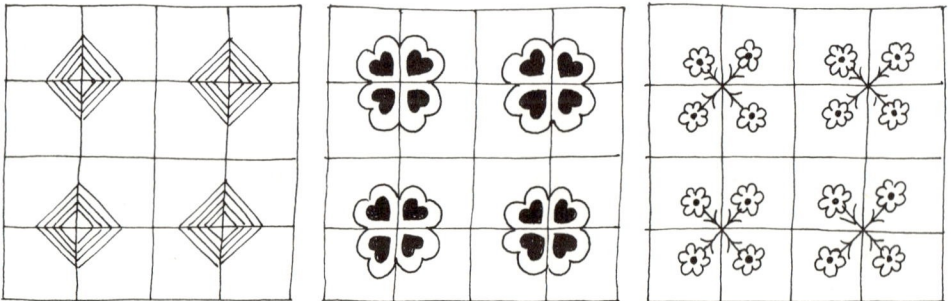

Second project

This is an elaboration of the first project, for which you should provide larger background papers, such as construction paper 12" x 18" (30 x 45 cm).

TEACHER PREPARATION

1. Cut light-colored paper into a lot of 1½" (4 cm) squares.

CREATING TILE PATTERNS

2. Let each student have at least 16 squares, but this time decorate two opposite corners with two different designs.

3. Ask students to arrange the tiles in a pleasing arrangement. It can be as large as they like, or in the form of a strip or a frame.

4. Let students experiment with creating many different tile patterns and find out what happens when the same designs are repeated on two corners; when designs are placed on all four corners of the square; and what effects geometric and realistic patterns produce.

VARIATIONS

Different sizes: Tiles can of course be made smaller or larger. Small tiles can be used for decorating report covers, gift boxes, and other small items. With large tiles, background scenery for school-plays can be made.

Mosaics: Plain tiles can be interspersed with decorated ones. Rings of concentric squares may appear.

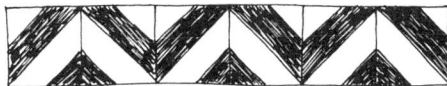

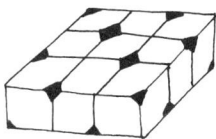

Christmas/Hanukkah Gift Exchange

Many adults spend a great deal of time and thought in making handcrafted Christmas and Hanukkah gifts, which they feel are more personal than purchased gifts. One of the by-products is a feeling of satisfaction when contemplating a completed wooden toy or knitted Santa Claus ornament.

Your students can reap that good feeling of accomplishment with a Christmas/Hanukkah Gift Exchange, in which they exchange names and make stuffed felt ornaments for each other. This simple sewing project is suitable for boys and girls. After all, needlework is no longer stereotyped and considered "sissy," for girls only. Well-known men in public life and the sports world have expressed their enjoyment of needlework.

This project calls for making stuffed felt ornaments. Felt is the easiest fabric for a beginner to handle, and it does not fray. School suppliers sell 9" x 12" pieces and some offer very inexpensive bags of scraps. Phun Phelt can also be used. One bag of stuffing from the dime store will be more than enough for your whole class, but you can also ask students to contribute leftover stuffing from home. Crushed plastic packing pebbles or snipped-up pieces of fabric can serve as stuffing substitutes.

Any kind of paper is suitable for drawing preliminary patterns.

MATERIALS

Felt pieces
Thread
Needles
Straight pins
Scissors

Drawing paper
Pencils
Stuffing
White glue
A box (or a hat)

INITIATING THE EXCHANGE

1. Let students write their names on individual pieces of paper. Put them in a box (or hat) and shake them up. Hold it above eye level and let each student pick out a name. If a child picks his/her own name, he/she takes out another piece of paper and returns the first name to the box. The child should keep the name tag he/she has drawn from the box and later on attach it to the completed gift.

2. Tell students they are going to make a felt ornament for the person whose name they picked. They should try to make something appropriate, if possible. For example, for a baseball player make a round ornament decorated to look like a baseball. Otherwise sew seasonal ornaments for Christmas and Hanukkah.

3. Decide with your class when they want to have the actual exchange. Should the ornaments all be kept in a box until the last day of school before Christmas vacation? If you have Jewish children in your class, consider the date of Hanukkah. Also decide whether or not the gifts should be wrapped.

HOW TO MAKE PAPER PATTERNS

1. Let students draw an outline of the "stuffy" they wish to make. Animals are okay, but narrow legs are difficult to handle. The illustrations show some designs that you can show your class, either as they appear in this book or as you reproduce them on the chalkboard. Also inspect the completed designs and suggest changes if outlines look too elaborate.

2. Cut out the paper patterns.

 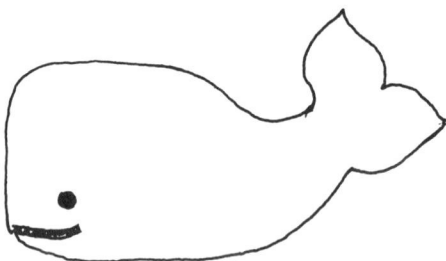 

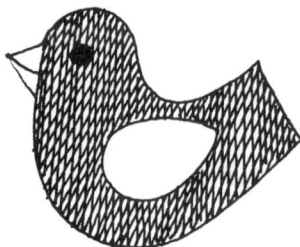  

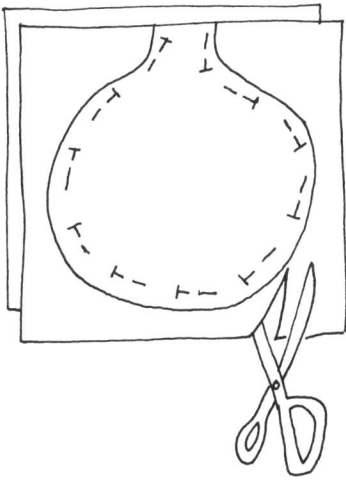

SEWING

3. Pin the paper pattern on *two* layers of felt and cut it out. Discard paper pattern.

4. Thread a needle. Young children may need a little help here and you may want to prepare threaded needles in advance. Also knot the ends of the thread.

5. Take three or four stitches through both layers; then pull the thread through. Continue this procedure.

6. Sew the two pieces of felt together, leaving a 2″ (5 cm) opening. Running stitch is best as it can be done from first grade up.

7. Push stuffing through the opening, making sure it reaches all corners.

8. Sew up the 2″ (5 cm) opening.

DECORATING

9. Small pieces of felt can be glued on. Use the scrap pieces left over from cutting out the basic shapes. Use white glue, sparingly, as felt tends to stick together on its own, anyway. Felt saturated with too much glue looks icky.

VARIATIONS

Christmas balls: You can have the whole class cut out two felt circles, stuff them, and then decorate them as Christmas balls.

Names: Block letters can be cut out of felt and glued onto the "stuffies."

Hangers: You can staple loops of string to the ornaments, ready for hanging on the tree.

Cut-outs: You can eliminate the stuffing and just have students cut out flat designs which they decorate. If felt is hard to come by, use construction paper instead.

Anything goes: Students can have a gift exchange with drawings, painted boxes, or valentines. In fact, any other art project can become the subject for a gift exchange. And you don't have to wait for Christmas!

Designing Record Covers

Have your students ever thought about designing record covers? This can be a popular project, and an introduction to the world of commercial art. Make them aware of the fact that artists can be paid for their talents, but they have to fulfill tasks set by an employer. Imagine that today's task is to design record covers.

MATERIALS

Drawing paper
Poster paints

THE PROJECT

1. Let students invent titles for records, such as "Love Songs from the Heart," by Pink Porky; or "Spring Training," by the Base Hits. You can write the suggested titles on the blackboard and let students select the ones they want to illustrate.

2. Students outline squares the same size as record albums—12½" x 12½" (32 x 32 cm).

3. Now they are ready to design the covers. Suggest that they first recall some of their favorite covers and think about why they like them.

4. When students have finished painting the covers, initiate a discussion about some attractive features and why some designs tell the message well.

VARIATIONS

Singles: Students design covers for single records instead of album size.

Pairing off: Students can pair off and suggest titles to each other.

Limitations: Normally it is a good idea for students' imaginations to fly freely, but you can set a specific goal, one of which is shown in the illustrations. These examples show repetitive patterns incorporated in the designs.

K-Grade 6

Scrappies

Children always enjoy cutting and pasting. The game of "Scrappies" involves collage, which will help them develop their sense of design and color. You can provide art papers or any other kind of colored paper—even scraps. Don't overlook old magazines as a varied source of patterns; under "Variations" you will find a good hint for making special use of them.

The project can take up a whole art period or be used as a short fill-in at different times.

MATERIALS

Colored paper scraps
Background paper
Scissors
Glue

HOW TO PLAY THE GAME

1. Each child cuts and glues three different paper shapes onto the background, fairly far apart.
2. The background papers are passed to the person on the left, who must make three separate pictures by cutting and gluing on more paper shapes.
3. Repeat the game several times.

VARIATIONS

Scenes: The three scrappies are to be combined into one complete picture. This is more complex and may not be suitable for lower grades. In any case it is best played after the regular version.

Specifics: Once your students have caught on to the game, they can decide that the scrappies must be turned into animals, or flowers, or any other category.

Magazine cut-outs: If a magazine page contains a patterned area that you think would be effective in a collage, placing a temporary frame around the area in question helps you to visualize its possibilities. For this purpose, cut two L-shaped pieces of cardboard. They can be shifted to encompass small or large areas. Pictures as well as print areas can be selected.

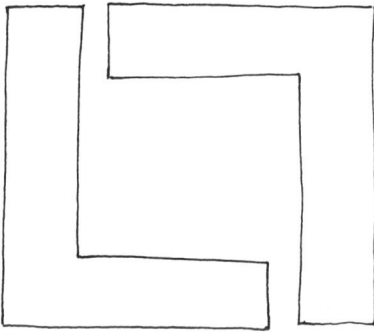

Chapter

Markers

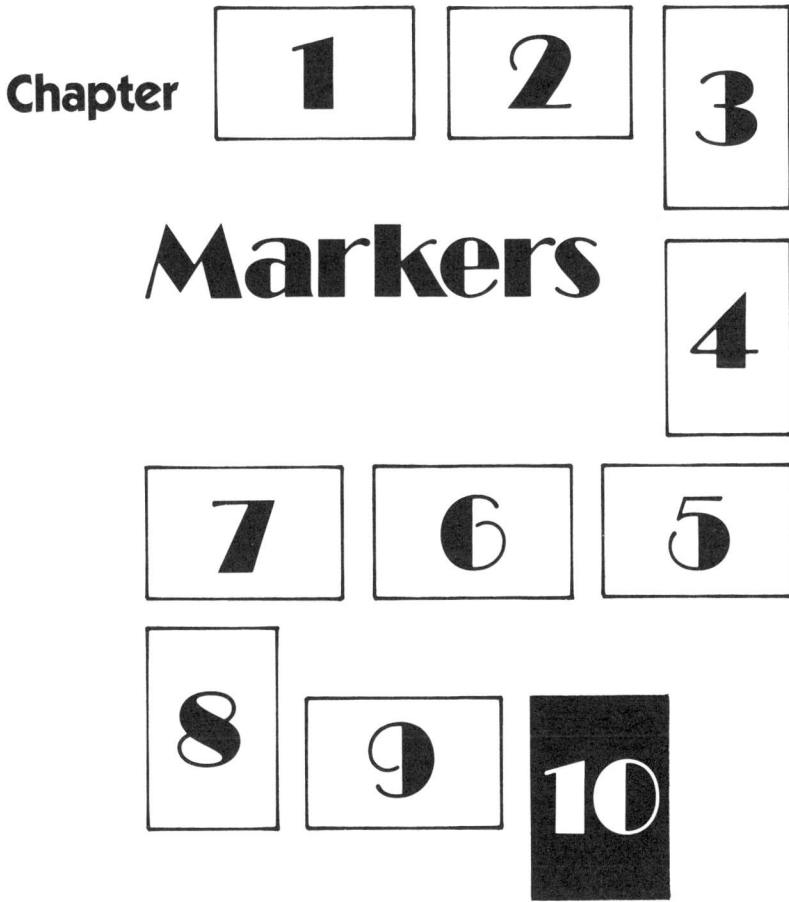

How to make markers for all sorts of games

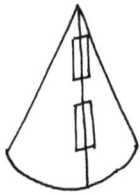

Markers

Many games require markers, perhaps only one for each player as in "On the Way to School," or 12 as in checkers. Markers can be distinguished by color or shape, or by both, and they have to be small enough to fit the spaces on the playing board. Beyond that the sky is the limit.

Here are a few ideas, some of which even offer a good chance to serve as an interesting art project for a whole period. Before starting make sure you have enough material in one color to make the required number of markers, and that students understand they have to repeat designs distinctly to make it easy for players to pick out their own markers.

Colored cardboard shapes

Cut squares and circles from different colored cardboard. If this is not available, glue colored paper to any kind of cardboard before cutting out.

Cardboard stand-ups

Interlock two pieces of cardboard with the slit and slot method (see drawing).

Graduated styrofoam forms

Collect a lot of styrofoam meat trays in different colors. Let students cut them up into geometric shapes in graduated sizes and glue them on top of each other with white glue.

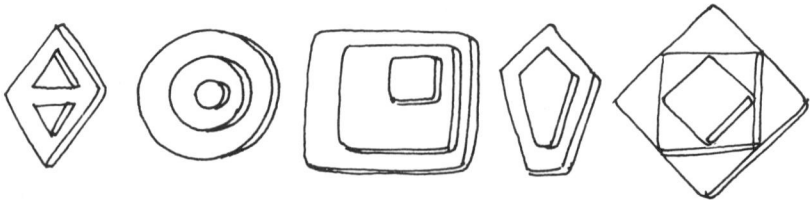

Bottle caps

Ask students to bring in bottle caps and make sure that none of them have acquired sharp edges in opening. Bottle caps can be used the way they are by sorting them into different kinds. Red caps contrast nicely with lemon/lime. They can also be painted all over in one color or with simple lines.

Pebbles

Ask your class to bring in pebbles, but take time to discuss what kinds of pebbles are most suitable. (They must fit on game boards and should not roll.) Wash and dry them. Students paint them with bold stripes—crosswise, lengthwise, and on the diagonal. Let them discover that repeated designs unify the irregularity of the pebbles.

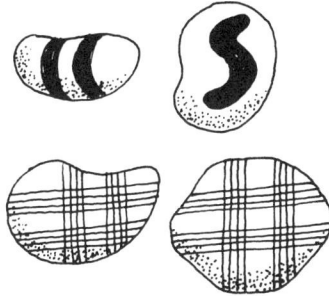

Shell markers

If your school is near a beach, ask students to bring in common shells. They should be small enough to fit on the board and can be used as they are or painted, depending on the type of shells available and the requirements of the game.

Nuts and bolts

Raid the home toolbox for nuts and bolts. Screw two nuts on one bolt and paint the tops in different colors.

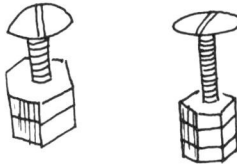

"Cookie" markers

Let students cut out bold shapes from styrofoam, then paint or glue on decorations. It's like cutting out Christmas cookies.

Holiday markers

Markers made with many of the methods described here can be adapted as a holiday project: hearts and arrows for Valentine's Day; stars and stripes for the Fourth of July; witches and goblins for Halloween; six-pointed stars and *dreidls* for Hanukkah; bells and trees for Christmas.

Dried vegetables

Many games were originally played with beans and other natural markers. Consider acorns, eucalyptus seed pods, walnut shells and horse chestnuts. They can be left in their natural state or painted.

Molecules

Decorate markers with scientific symbols.

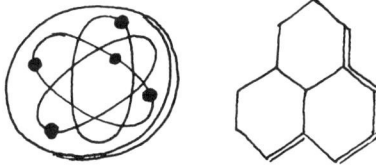

Clay markers

Any kind of clay can be used. Unless your school has a kiln, consult your school supplies catalog for self-hardening clay, or the kind that can be baked in a regular oven. If this is your students' first encounter with clay, suggest that they begin making sausages and disks, which they can combine into different forms.

Sausages are made by rolling a small amount of clay into a sausage, which can be thick or thin, short or long. A sausage can be curled up or several sausages can be combined into a person or an animal.

Disks are made by rolling a small quantity of clay into a ball and flattening it. Balls and disks can be combined.

Textured markers

Clay markers can be scratched with toothpicks, forks, and other tools.

Origami markers

Fold paper into simple shapes.

Lifesavers

Glue paper reinforcement circles onto pieces of cardboard.

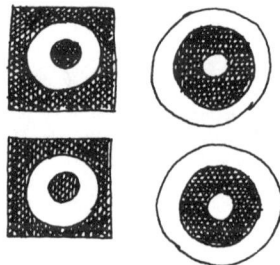

Faces

Draw faces on cardboard circles.

Cones

Cut paper into semi-circles and roll into a cone. Glue or tape the straight edges together.

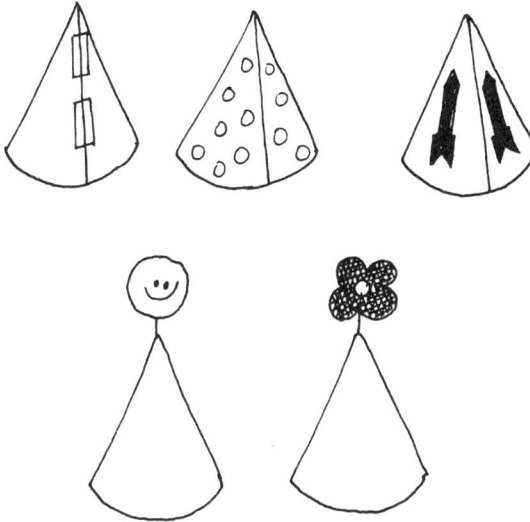

Self-stick markers

Find self-stick plastic (Con-Tact®) with repetitive patterns. Apply to cardboard and then cut out individual designs.

Pennies

Pennies can be used for markers. One person uses heads and the other tails. An even better way is to place paper over coins and rub over it with a soft pencil.

The moon and the stars

One player draws moons on his/her markers and the other draws stars.

Sponge

Cut sponges into all kinds of shapes.

Acrylic

Drop acrylic modeling paste onto waxed paper, where it will spread into free-form shapes. While it is still wet, press small odds and ends into it. Paint with acrylic colors and shine with gloss medium. It makes a really great art project.

Index

4232-2
5-14